LEE WULFF
ON FLIES

LEE WULFF ON FLIES

Stackpole Books

799.12
WUL

LEE WULFF ON FLIES
Copyright © 1980 by Lee Wulff

Published by
STACKPOLE BOOKS
Cameron and Kelker Streets
P.O. Box 1831
Harrisburg, Pa. 17105

Published simultaneously in Don Mills, Ontario, Canada by Thomas Nelson & Sons, Ltd.

Cover photograph by Cris Lee.

"Scissors on the Stream" reprinted from Sports Afield magazine — June 1979 issue. Copyright © 1979 The Hearst Corporation. All rights reserved.

Printed in the U.S.A. .

Library of Congress Cataloging in Publication Data

Wulff, Lee.
    Lee Wulff on flies.

    Includes index.
    1. Fly fishing.   2. Flies, Artificial.   3. Fly
    tying.   I. Title.
SH456.W84 1979   688.7'9   79-5028
ISBN 0-8117-0953-1

Dedicated to all the inquisitive anglers, past, present and future, who have made and will make fly-fishing an intriguing, ever-challenging lifetime sport

Contents

Preface   9

ONE   Beginnings   11
TWO   What Makes a Fish Take a Fly?   21
THREE   Matching the Hatch   31
FOUR   A Basic Assortment of Trout Flies   45
FIVE   The Wulff Flies   53
SIX   Spiders and Skaters   63
SEVEN   Streamers   73
EIGHT   Special Flies   85
              Flexible Flies
              Backward Dry Flies
              Looped-Hackle Flies
              The Wretched Mess
              Form-A-Lure Plastic-Bodied Flies
NINE   Flies for Bass and Lake Fishes   115
TEN   Saltwater Flies   123
ELEVEN   Choosing Atlantic Salmon Flies   131
TWELVE   Thoughts on Flies and Fly-Fishing   145
          Index   157

Preface

This is a book on understanding what an artificial fly can represent, what it should look like and why it may be attractive to a fish. It is not a book on how to tie or make flies, although it shows how some flies are made and what goes into making a good one. This book shows how to put flies in their proper categories as imitations, and it shows how to cover a wide range of stream, lake and ocean life with a minimum of fly changes. It is as much a book on fishing as it is a book on flies. I hope it helps the reader to better understand how a fish looks at a fly and, understanding that, become a better fisherman. Most of the flies described in this book are flies that I originated, and I am very happy that I've been able to create flies that appeal to fish.

Any basic book on flies should, I believe, find its roots in the field of trout fishing. Trout flies have a history going back to the Romans and perhaps the ancient Egyptians. Trout fishing was the

9

first recognized angling sport, and perhaps this was because of the magic of the trout-stream insects. These insects, of which there are literally thousands of different species, start out as underwater creatures possessed of the fantastic ability to change, sometimes in only an instant, from a living submarine to a living, flying airplane. They are unique to the streams and fresh waters. Nowhere in the sea is there anything like the hatches of the trout streams, where hordes of insects of a given type or types leave the water to fly in the air above. After a short airborne life cycle these stream insects come back to the water to lay their eggs and, often, to fall dead to the surface to drift with the currents over the trout.

Trout may learn to be very selective, choosing to feed at any given time only on one particular insect that happens to appeal to their taste at that moment. The problem of what insect to match or what fly to use to match it has intrigued rich and poor, king and commoner, for generation after generation. Each new day becomes a different challenge, each season a new and complex series of problems, each decade a story of varied successes and failures and of always trying to attain the impossible dream: perfection in angling.

The fly tier may find new and stimulating ideas about his craft in this book. The angler who does not tie flies can use it as a guide in his choice of flies. It is my hope that both will learn to select flies by their look, learning to picture them in or on the water. I hope that they will see in flies the particular things that appeal to fish and, as their experience grows, also appeal to them.

ONE

Beginnings

I guess fishing came as naturally to me as walking. According to my mother I started both at about the same time. We lived in a small house next to the Tillicum Club in Valdez, Alaska, and a small brook ran past the back of the house. I was born in 1905, and by the time I was two I was catching trout on a piece of bacon and a bent pin. I loved water from the start and was always as close to it as I could get. The best thing about water, as far as I was concerned, was the fish that were in it. Catching those fish was more fun than anything else I did.

Valdez was a frontier mining town and a jumping-off place for the interior of Alaska. The trout and salmon runs in the nearby rivers were fantastic. During the runs the salmon were so crowded in the streams that they could be taken with spears, snares, gaffs or big treble snagging hooks. They could even be hit and stunned with the pick-poles that were normally used to push logs and small boats around. Anything short of dynamite was legal, and I learned all the different ways of catching fish.

In Valdez it seemed there were as many dogs as there were people—maybe more. There were big dogs from Iditarod and small dogs from Nome. They were of all shapes and dispositions, but they all had one thing in common: They were all hungry. In the winter they were well fed so that they could work hard pulling the sleds. In the summer, when the sleds were put aside, the dogs were almost as hungry as they were in the winter, but no one wanted to pay for their food. The cheapest thing they could live on was fish. Slop Jack, a sort of town indigent who carried away the trash from the saloons, had the contract to feed them. I was his helper. What could be more wonderful for a kid fishing freak than to go fishing every day with no limit and an endless demand for the fish?

I liked spearing best. You had to spot the fish and perhaps stalk it a bit before you made your strike with the spear. That meant you had to learn where the fish usually rested, where they fed and where they hid. When the fish were racing downstream in the current, spearing called for a good eye and a good arm.

When the salmon runs were on trout were easy to catch with fishing tackle, using salmon eggs as bait. But they weren't so easy when only the resident fish or the few early salmon were in the streams, and only one angler in town used flies to catch them. Rosy Roseen, a misplaced Englishman and a jail guard at the local klink, had a fly rod and flies, and I tagged along to see how he caught trout.

When I was nine my father, who didn't give a hoot about fishing himself, sent away for a fly-fishing outfit for me. There were only a few flies with it, and I soon lost them. Because Rosy had only a few himself, I tried to make flies. I tied them clumsily in my fingers with any feathers I could find—from robin feathers to raven feathers—holding the flies together with silk from my mother's sewing basket. I remember pulling fibers from hackle-type feathers and spreading them evenly around the fly in an effort to imitate the flies pictured in the catalogs. Perhaps you can imagine the wonder with which, after we had moved to New York, I first watched a fly tier take hackle pliers in hand and spin a hackle around a hook shank to make that beautiful flare of feather fibers!

Fooling the fish with something artificial intrigued me. Already hooked on fishing, I became hooked on fishing with flies. I learned to tie flies completely with my fingers, because I knew nothing of fly-tying vises, hackle pliers and other such things at the time. Having started that way I've continued right on tying flies by hand for a lifetime, making everything from tandem 4/0 flies for marlin to #28 flies for trout. There is a knack to it that I learned young, and I feel that I tie flies faster and just as securely as if they were tied in a vise.

To tie most flies I grip the eye of the hook firmly between the nails of my left forefinger and thumb. It is a secure hold—just as steady as a vise. With my right hand I wind the thread, keeping tension on it at all times and throwing a half hitch or two over the work to hold the thread in position if I have to put the fly down for any reason.

In 1920, when I was fifteen, we moved from New York to California. I knew there would be a lot of trout out west, and I saved all of my school lunch money, augmenting that fund by doing odd jobs whenever I could. In late spring I got on my bicycle and pedaled some six miles to lower Manhattan to the store of Abbey & Imbrie, whose catalog was tops among those I had dreamed over all winter. I entered the store with over thirty dollars in my pocket, and I came out with a lot of tackle and no money. I had a new fly rod, reel and line, a landing net and a lot of fly-tying materials. I had Lollacapop fly dope, hooks, sinkers, leaders, Colorado spinners and rubber worms and crickets. I had feathers from birds from far-off parts of the world, and most importantly I had the small, very stiff hackles that were needed for tying dry flies.

We spent two weeks in Yosemite National Park on that trip west. The fishing was marvelous. I had to put in a day or two with my family seeing the sights—the big sequoia trees you could drive a car through, the waterfalls that dropped hundreds of feet, the great cliffs and domes—that make that park more breathtaking than any other. Then, while my father and mother and two sisters enjoyed what everyone else was enjoying—from tennis to the evening fire fall, when the flaming embers of a big bonfire were pushed over the edge of a cliff—I went fishing.

I was up at dawn, wearing cotton pants and sneakers, climbing the trail past the Vernal and Nevada falls to the upper Merced River. I don't remember seeing another fisherman there. I waded wet and cast my dry flies as the magazines said they should be cast. The rainbows obliged often enough to keep me interested through the long hours until twilight. Then I'd race back down the trail to our tent in the campground on the valley floor, bringing the bigger fish that I had caught.

My mother had insisted, when I refused to take any sandwiches with me, that I take along two little packages of Sunkist raisins, just in case I got hungry. The first day I forgot all about the raisins, and when I sat down for supper I pulled them out of my pocket to eat with dessert. I quickly learned to eat them somewhere along the trail on the way home from the high river so my mother wouldn't worry about my starving to death.

One day, while fishing the big Merced River at the lower end of the valley, I found some good fish rising that I couldn't catch. The fish of the upper river hadn't minded that my leader was probably 2X or thicker, or that my flies were tied on #12 hooks or larger. But these fish were smart enough to make a fool of me. I got a little frustrated, and I guess it showed in my casting.

The highway ran right along the river, and cars often stopped to watch a fisherman. Usually they stayed only a minute or two. If I hooked a fish they stayed until it was landed or lost and then drove on. But this time a car door slammed, and a man came walking down over the rocks to the water's edge. I turned to face him, and he beckoned. I stopped fishing and waded to shore to talk to him.

He held a little box out to me. I took it and looked inside: In it were two of the smallest flies I had ever seen. They were dry flies that looked just like real mosquitoes. I didn't know it at the time, but they were #16 Quill Gordons.

"I think they'll do the trick," he said. "I just happened to have a couple of extras, and I think you need them more than I do," and he turned to go.

"What's your name, sir?" I called after him. "I could let you know how I made out."

"My name," he said, "is Outdoor Franklin. Good luck!" Then he was gone, scrambling up the bank and over the rocks to his car and driving off as if he were late for an important appointment.

A couple of rainbows did come up and look at that #16 fly, but they turned away short of taking it. Perhaps if the man had given me a long, fine leader tippet as well as the flies I could have fooled those trout. Later, after we had settled in San Diego, I learned that Outdoor Franklin wrote a hunting and fishing column for one of the Los Angeles newspapers, and I wrote him a letter about his flies with my thanks.

There was great fishing in the West then. I fished the Rogue and the Klamath rivers, and during a summer vacation from college in 1923 I fished in Alaska again, between driving a truck

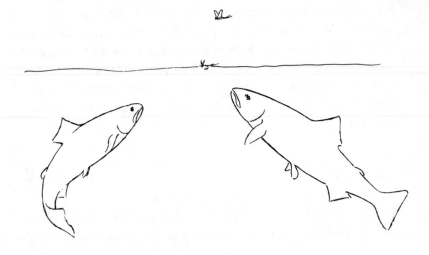

over the highway from Valdez to Fairbanks and working as a stevedore on the docks at Valdez. Then along came girls, and I neglected my fishing. I finished engineering school at Stanford University, went to Paris to study art and came back to New York to get started in commercial art, my chosen field.

After a year in New york I met Walter Grotz, an artist in the advertising agency for which I was an art director. Walter was a dedicated angler—a trout fisherman who worked, ate and slept only to fish. I had given away or sold all my guns and fishing tackle in San Diego before going to Europe, and I hadn't fished since. But Walter's enthusiasm rekindled mine, and I bought a new fly-fishing outfit. Soon I found myself spending a Saturday wading and casting to trout in New Jersey's Saddle River, which was close to Walter's home.

From then on practically every weekend of the season found me on a trout stream. With Bela Dankovsky, another artist and fisherman, Walter and I fished the streams within reach of New York City, especially the Catskill streams. On my vacations I went up to Byron Blanchard's fishing inn on the East Branch of New York's Ausable, in the Adirondack Mountains, a place where such fishing greats as George LaBranche and Ray Bergman went to fish.

I had become used to improvising when I fished in the West, and I began to improvise with flies on these famous trout waters of the East. Walter and I had been looking under rocks and in the moss to find what food there was in the streams for the trout. We took caddis worms out of their little wooden houses and hung them, two to a hook, on a #14 hook and drifted them through the pocket waters with excellent results. We hooked stonefly nymphs through the collar on #16 hooks, put a split-shot a foot above them on the leader, and let the current take them into the pockets and eddies where the trout were waiting. Those live stoneflies were truly deadly.

At that time Ray Bergman worked as a salesman in the William Mills & Sons tackle store on Park Place in lower Manhattan. Walter made up a caddis-worm imitation by wrapping

Top, caddis pupae, two to a book; *bottom,* a stonefly nymph hooked through the collar.

white chenille around the shank of a #12 hook and adding a few turns of peacock herl at the head. Of course, if you think about it, you realize that no soft, pearly-white caddis worm is likely to leave its protective stone or wooden case and come floating down the stream. But, although the trout may never have seen uncased caddis worms before, they knew instinctively what to do with them. They took them—and Walter's imitations—like a kid takes candy. Ray promised to try Walter's fly, and it later became the RB Caddis shown in the plates of Ray's great book, *Trout.*

Soon I was making imitation stonefly nymphs by sewing pieces of soft chamois into the proper shape and making legs with pieces of peacock herl and other things. Our imitations worked, and Walter and I took greater pleasure in catching fish on the imitations we had made than on the real things.

It was a time for experimenting. Ed Hewitt had come up with

The RB Caddis.

the Spider, which was immediately popular with the small group of trout fishermen who had gone to small hooks in their flies. Hewitt had also given us the Bivisible, which floated readily and high on the water while the other flies of the day did not. Bivisibles caught fish more consistently than any other pattern, it seemed.

I looked at the dry flies available at the time and found that they were always slim-bodied and sparsely hackled. They were made only of feathers, and they were hard to keep afloat. If a fish were caught on one of them, the fly had to be retired to dry a while before it would float again.

I wanted a buggier-looking, heavier-bodied fly, and I needed more flotation in order to keep it up. I had in mind the big gray drakes that came out on the Ausable, which were heavier in the body than any of the dry-fly imitations of the day. Looking for a material that would float such a body, I came up with bucktail. The tail of the fly was most important since it would support the bend of the hook, where most of the weight is concentrated. Bucktail would make a much better tailing material than the conventional feather fibers because of its floating qualities and its strength. The flotation of the old flies was mostly at the front, and the usual wisps of feather fibers wouldn't make a strong, floating tail. For example, the few golden-pheasant tippet-feather fibers of a Royal Coachman tail certainly didn't have enough strength to hold the hook bend up for very long.

Out of this thinking came the Gray Wulff, White Wulff and Royal Wulff. My use of bucktail was the first use of animal hair on dry flies. The Royal Wulff made the old, difficult-to-float, but beautiful, Royal Coachman pattern into a hell of a fly. The White

Wulff was tied to imitate the coffin mayfly. I tied it both conventionally and with spent wings and no hackle to match the flies of the spinner fall—when the mayflies, spent with mating, fall to the water with wings outspread. Had I been brighter I would have patented the use of animal hair on dry flies and made some money, but I feel lucky that through these flies my name achieved a permanent place in fly-fishing.

The Gray Wulff has brown bucktail wings and tail, blue-gray hackles and a gray angora yarn (spun rabbit's fur) body. The White Wulff has white bucktail wings and tail, badger hackles and cream-colored angora for the body. The Royal Wulff has white bucktail wings, brown bucktail tail, dark brown hackles and a body of red silk floss between two segments of wound peacock herl.

Dan Bailey, a close friend and one of my early fishing companions, insisted that I call the Gray Wulff by its present name instead of the Ausable Gray as I had thought to call it. It was Dan, who was beginning to tie and sell flies at that time, who sat down with me while we worked out the other patterns of the series to cover the field of trout-stream insects in general. The Grizzly Wulff, the Black Wulff, the Brown Wulff and the Blonde Wulff came out of those sessions.

Those were interesting days. In 1931 I had already designed and made the first fishing vest, and we were feeling our oats as fishermen. Dan and I decided to set up fishing classes, and our friend Ray Camp, outdoor writer for *The New York Times*, gave us a plug in his column. We invited John MacDonald, *Fortune* magazine writer and fishing friend, to come for free. When class

Fly on right has a bucktail tail, which floats it more naturally on the surface.

time came we had Ray, John, ourselves and one paying student! The student was John McCloy, who later became one of President Roosevelt's ace European diplomatic trouble-shooters during World War II. Whether most fishermen of the time felt they knew all they needed to know about fishing, or that we didn't know enough to teach them anything or that ten dollars a session was too much, I'm not sure.

It was not long after that endeavor with Dan Bailey that I wrote that a good gamefish is too valuable to be used only once. In 1960 I had the first network television show on fishing on the CBS "Sports Spectacular," and in 1964 I shifted to the ABC "American Sportsman" to make fishing films. I was able through these shows to give people a sense of sound conservation practices. They could see the fish caught and then see it released to swim away, and they could know that the fish was there for somebody else to catch.

In recent years we have seen the proliferation of no-kill areas and the growing practice of returning fish. There are also many more anglers. The fisherman of today has to be a lot more capable to be successful than the fisherman of the 1930s because the fish are a lot smarter, having been educated by being caught and released and by being fished for by more anglers.

At this writing my wife, Joan, and I are starting a fly-fishing school here on the Beaverkill River in the Catskills, where we now live. Joan is a former casting champion, and I know I've learned an awful lot more to teach than I knew when I embarked on that first teaching venture. Things have changed a lot since that first class with Dan Bailey forty-five years ago.

T W O

What Makes a
Fish Take a Fly?

Trout eat living things. Motion is a sign of life. A trout's instinct tells the trout that if something moves of its own volition it must have life, and, therefore, chances are it will be good to eat. All too often an angler thinks a trout took his fly because it was a particular blend of color and design, when actually that fish would have taken almost anything of about that size that was given the same motion.

Assuming a fly is within the correct size range, there are three basic things that influence its effectiveness. The first is the motion it can be given in or on the water. The second is the way it works on its own in or on the water. The third is the look of the fly itself.

Wrap a hook with a bit of yarn or put a little fragment of a red bandanna on a hook or tie a tiny bit of a green leaf on a small hook, and give it the action of a swimming or struggling bug, and it can draw a strike. Over a long fishing career I have caught trout on such things as a wild strawberry, a blueberry, a dandelion head, a fragment of rotted wood, a piece of carrot and a bare hook. A fish is curious, and if something of eating size comes along, it's quite reasonable that a fish should take it in its mouth to test its taste and texture. If the trout doesn't like it, it can always spit it out. This goes for relatively unsophisticated fish. Wise ones, which have been caught or hooked before, may be less anxious to experiment and may look for a leader to see whether or not that or some other connection is causing the motion that simulates life.

The first fly ever to fall into and move through a never-before-fished pool will be taken quickly by the nearest brook trout that can see it. Knowing where the best feeding spots will be, I have often cast a fly into a virgin pool in the North Country and taken the biggest fish in the pool on the first cast. The biggest fish pre-empt the best feeding spots and take first choice of the food. Fish learn to be cautious through experience and heredity. It is interesting that brown trout, which have been fished for for hundreds of years, tend to be born cautious. Our brook trout, on the other hand, have been fished for for a much shorter period of time, and they seem to be born with less caution and a greater, more consuming hunger.

The typical trout fly is an insect imitation. For a long time all trout flies were made to represent insects. The standard trout fly prior to the 1920s was a wet fly designed with feathered wings laid back at about a forty-five degree angle over the shank. The time-honored patterns in which these flies were tied, such as the Coachman, Royal Coachman, Lead-Wing Coachman, Black Gnat, Dark Montreal, Cowdung, Queen of the Waters, Parmachene Belle, Red Ibis, Yellow Sally, Professor, Orange Fish Hawk, Brown Hackle and Gray Hackle, all had wings like those that flying insects have—yet these flies were fished under the water like modern nymphs. The idea of retrieving a winged insect under the water seems strange to us now, and most of these flies have gone out of favor. Yet in spite of the incongruity, they still work. They work because they look like bugs and they *move*. I think more wet flies are taken by fish simply because they move than for any other reason, and it is very important for an angler to understand this.

Motion was the best thing the old-style wet flies had going for them. Most anglers twitched them a little to make them seem even more alive, even though they were pulled across and against the current and already had the basic semblance of life. Often a dropper fly was skimmed across the surface ahead of the tail fly, or flies, that swam under the surface. This skimming or dancing motion of the dropper often attracted trout that would not take the sunken fly, or flies.

Whether or not motion imparted by the angler, as the wet fly makes its traditional swing after a forty-five-degree cast downstream and across the current, is wise or essential is a matter of conjecture. Most trout fishermen impart an uneven swing to their flies by lifting and lowering their rods or by pulling line in unevenly on the retrieve. I use such an uneven retrieve for trout and feel it catches more fish for me than if I let the fly take a perfectly smooth swing.

Trout are more determined to take a fly than are salmon because the trout are actively feeding when the fly fisher is casting to them, and the salmon are not. There is great doubt that twitching the fly on the retrieve makes the fly more attractive to Atlantic salmon. I know many excellent salmon fishermen who use only one method or the other, and both groups seem equal in fishing ability. I choose to let my salmon wet flies make a smooth, uninterrupted swing. My reasoning is that since my flies are moving through the water they have the semblance of life, and if a salmon decides to investigate one with a smooth, even swing the salmon is less likely to miss it than he would be with a fly I was jerking unevenly through the water. With a trout I feel that the extra motion is more noticeable and can be interpreted as an excited effort to escape.

With nymphs a free drift is the accepted fashion, but an occasional small twitch—just enough to affirm life—is my

choice. Some natural nymphs have poor swimming ability; others can swim like small minnows. It pays to know which ones do what.

Dry flies are normally drifted freely, yet signs of life are worthwhile on some imitations. A grasshopper may kick its legs violently after it has landed on the water. A bee or moosefly on the water may buzz around in circles. A moth may flutter wildly, although moving little. A stonefly may drift freely, yet squirm a little as it readies itself for flight again. Motion is one of the fly fisherman's main tools, and it should be used with understanding.

Rubber crickets and worms have been on the market since I was in knee pants. They look just like the real things. The trouble is they don't work very well. Being of stiff, solid rubber they have little or no motion within themselves. The soft tendrils of feather or fur on a less-than-perfect imitation give a look of life, I believe, that is more important to the fish than a perfect but lifeless image. Something that looks exactly like a bug is not as effective as something that may look less like one but *acts* more like a bug in the movements it makes by itself.

In making flies the things in my mind are both the general appearance and the way the fly will work as I fish it. I tie some flies with maribou-like feathers, the softest possible, so they will have a lifelike look even when they are barely moving. There will be others that I will want to hold their shape well when moved through fast water. Wild brook trout, for example, are greatly attracted to a fluffy Spider fished underwater with short jerks. The Spider's fan of hackle fibers, alternately bending and returning, makes the fly look more like a jellyfish than like an insect. I've tried the same stunt with brown trout and almost always been ignored. Fishing a Spider underwater is something the fishing books do not suggest, but, at least on wild brookies, it can be a smart way to fish.

Every time I look at side-by-side comparison photographs of a real insect and the artificial that supposedly imitates it, I'm struck by their dissimilarity. If you didn't know that trout will often take *that* artificial when feeding on *that* natural, you wouldn't think the two looked at all alike, except perhaps for color. The real one has a few wisps, not more than three, for a tail; the artificial may have several times as many. The real insect's wings slant in one direction; the imitation's wings often slant in a different direction. There is such a difference between an insect and the fly that works in its stead that one comes to the conclusion

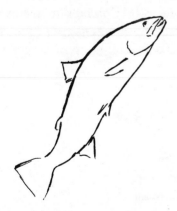

that there is a great deal of illusion in the way trout look at things as well as in the way anglers look at things.

Generally speaking, dry flies must be much better imitations of insects than wet flies. Wet flies have the advantage of having motion through the water to give them the semblance of life. A dry fly floats along without motion, except for an occasional twitch with some patterns, and it must distinguish itself by its insectlike shape from the floating bits of leaves and twigs and other flotsam that trout recognize as inedible and leave alone.

Most fishermen, having read the books, magazines and catalogs, have a picture in their minds of what they think a successful fly should look like. This is a dangerous trap for an angler to fall into because once the angler decides that certain, particular patterns are what the trout want and that others won't do, his mind becomes closed to a lot of possibilities.

Back in the early 1930s, when I was tying flies commercially to augment my meager income and fill in the times when, as a freelance artist, I couldn't find work to do, I tied a lot of Wulff flies and did a lot of fishing all through the season. On the Battenkill one of my most successful flies was a nymph tied with gray angora wool on a #10 hook with a couple of turns of peacock herl at the head and a touch at the tail. It was simply a Gray Wulff body with the peacock herl to give it a little character. When I didn't put the herl head on, it didn't seem to make any difference. I fished it most often as a dropper ahead of a streamer.

At that time I was selling the standard dry flies for twenty-five cents each, and I tried to sell my best customers some of my gray nymphs, giving these customers a special price of fifteen cents

The Gray Nymph.

each because the flies were so simple to tie. I couldn't sell them. My customers didn't feel that enough work had been put into the flies. Therefore, my customers weren't interested and felt the trout wouldn't be either.

Forty years later at a Fario Club dinner in Paris hosted by Charlie Ritz, I met famed English fisherman and riverkeeper Frank Sawyer. From a little box that he carried in the pocket of his tweed coat, Sawyer displayed a bunch of gray-bodied nymphs that were almost identical to the ones I'd made up for my own use back in those Depression days. Taking one out to give me, he said, "These are wonderful nymphs. I think they're the best all-around flies there are for trout."

With our modern anglers' deepening interest in the stream insects there has come a tendency to make up exact replicas of the insects. They are beautiful works of art. They speak highly of the skill of the tier. They have an exciting look for the fishermen. They look like the real thing, but unless an angler is experienced, he'll fish them hard and get poor results. I think they should be mounted and hung on the wall, or simply carried about as I carry some of the magnificent old Scottish salmon patterns just for the pleasure of having them with me, taking them out to use only occasionally when my standby flies fail to bring any action. The trouble is that the exact imitations may have the static look of the real things, but usually they don't *act* like the real things.

I have always taken the position that fancy feathers do not catch more fish. In the heyday of British fly-fishing, tiers scoured the world for special feathers. Flies were tied precisely to pattern by the top tiers, without varying as much as a single fiber. The patterns I tie are created from ordinary materials readily at hand. The Wulff series is tied with the simplest things. I use dyed blue-dun hackles for the Gray Wulff, being interested in the color rather than the lineage of the rooster that provided the hackles. How in the world can a trout that has never been out of his stream tell whether a fly is made with a true Andalusian blue hackle from far-off Spain or from an ordinary local rooster butchered in Brooklyn and dyed about the same color? I don't believe he can. I use dyed hackles when they're easier to get than natural colors. I use any available material that will give the effect and look I want and also have the maximum durability for hard fishing.

There is a growing difficulty in getting the fine feathers that for years have been standbys in the most beautiful of fly patterns. With the increasing protection of wild birds, we who tie flies are more and more limited to those animals and birds that are either raised for food or are considered fair game for hunters. This will affect the looks of flies greatly and will take away much of the charm of some patterns. It will be a real loss for those anglers who have great memories of the old patterns taking fish under difficult circumstances.

Whether or not it will have any effect on fishing is debatable. Some of the most effective flies, such as the Blue Charm, March Brown and Silver Blue, are simple flies and can be made with readily available materials. I was in Newfoundland when the ban on importing jungle-cock neck feathers went through. A wail went up from most salmon fishermen. A few felt that without jungle-cock "eyes" (a term suggested by the color pattern on each hackle) their flies would not be effective. In my usual disturbing fashion in such matters, I bet that I could catch as many salmon on flies without jungle-cock eyes as each of them would average on flies with jungle-cock eyes. They didn't bet, but we kept track, and we found that they would have lost.

Sheer beauty in human eyes won't catch trout and salmon, but I'm sure it will always be a great satisfaction for an angler to know that his flies are as beautiful as man can make them.

Although we tend to agree that deer and most other animals can't distinguish colors, we anglers tend to agree that fish can. Therefore we use color in our flies in a way that pleases us or seems natural to us. The evidence that fish see color just as we do is not conclusive. How many blushing faces do you think there would be among us if a new scientific study were to come out with proof that fish have little or no color perception? We have certainly spent a lot of time and money on our lures on the premise that fish see color much as we do. Let's try, then, to assess the value of color in our flies.

Many of us see the value as limited. I know an old angler who made all his flies in black and white and the gray shades in between. He was a successful angler and scoffed at those who used color. I believe that most experienced fishermen think more in terms of the density of the color rather than its brilliance, of its shading between black and white rather than its components of red, yellow and blue. I have a friend who is color-blind. He distinguishes red lights readily enough when driving, but as a shade of gray. He has no problem driving in traffic. I wonder if fish see color in some such abnormal—to us—way?

It is reasonable to rely more on shade than color brilliance to tempt our fish. We've all had times when a certain color in a fly seemed to make the difference between getting strikes and not getting strikes. We'll never know, however, whether or not some particular shade of gray would have looked the same to the fish and worked as well. Bass lures have gone to colors that all anglers would have shied away from not many years ago. They are being made in wild colors, such as chartreuse and cerise, even though anglers know a bass never saw a living thing wearing those colors. I've taken many fish on colors that, to the traditionally minded angler, would seem useless.

I think of color in flies as a matter of artistic pleasure and fun for the angler rather than as a necessity for the catching of fish. It is fun to use color, and it does help us tell our flies apart more easily than if they were all just shades of gray.

What makes a fish take a fly? It takes a fly because the fly looks like something to eat. And the fly looks like something to eat if it combines the elements of size, motion (imparted by the angler or within itself) and insectlike appearance. In the next chapter we'll look at how to imitate specific insects and the problem of fishing for selectively feeding trout.

THREE

Matching the Hatch

Matching the hatch is the hard core of dry-fly fishing for trout. Sometimes it is easy to match the hatch, but often it is a bewildering problem. Many books have been written on the topic, and it has caused more fishermen to learn about aquatic insect life and trout-stream ecology than anything else could have. There is magic and wonder and excitement when a hatch comes on, and those fishermen who have yet to see fish feeding on clouds of hatching or returning stream insects have missed what may be the most exciting moments of trout fishing.

Matching the hatch is basically easy to understand. It is something the angler can see: He can study the stream's surface, identify the hatch or hatches in progress and select from his flies. He may not know the names of the bugs, but he can see their shape, size and color.

In addition to trying to match the hatch, the angler will also be struggling to have his leader fine enough to fool the fish and to have his never-quite-perfect imitation float on the water in a manner identical to the natural. Sometimes the angler will be faced with the problem of having thousands of natural insects coming down the river, and he might despair about the chances of his fly being chosen by the trout he sees rising. Sometimes the flies will be so thick that there will be dozens to the square foot of stream surface. Why should any trout take an angler's imperfect imitation when there are real insects within an inch or two of the imitation? The fish naturally takes the real flies almost exclusively unless there is something especially attractive about the artificial—perhaps it is slightly larger, lower floating or has a brighter color than the natural. The real key to success, however, is putting the fly in the perfect spot just as the trout is moving up for its next mouthful—something that calls for sensing the rhythm of the rise and may depend as much on luck as on skill.

We will not go into the myriad different hatches that occur and the artificials that imitate them. Many fly patterns are named after the insects they are designed to imitate, and vice versa. Quill Gordon, Hendrickson, Cahill, Blue Dun, Pale Evening Dun and a host of other names are often used interchangeably to refer to the insect or the artificial. But we will briefly go into the charac-teristics of the basic stream insects that trout feed on. These are the mayflies, caddisflies, stoneflies, midges and terrestrials.

The freshly hatched mayfly rides the water with its wings together in an upright position like a little sailboat. Its first flying, or semi-adult, stage is the dun. The dun is usually soft in looks and texture with reasonably opaque wings. In a day or two it molts, and its wings become almost completely transparent and its body smoother and shinier than in the dun stage. This is the mature insect and is called the spinner stage. The mayfly is then ready to return to the stream to mate. After the mating flights over the stream and egg laying, the mayfly falls to the water with wings spread out on either side of the body and floats lifeless on the surface.

Through custom by fishermen and acceptance by the trout,

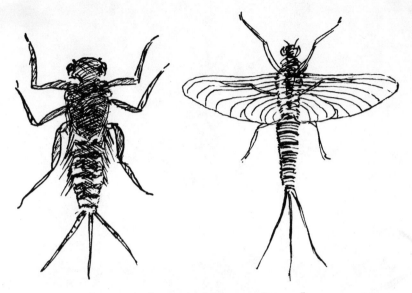

Left, mayfly nymph; *right,* spent-wing mayfly.

the wings of the dun mayfly are separated on such patterns as the Blue Dun, Quill Gordon, Hendrickson and others. But a single wing in the plane through which the hook shank passes would be a much better imitation, I think. I'm willing to bet that such a wing would catch as many or more fish than the conventional split wings. I make some flies with such a single wing and find them effective. But put them in a store and people, who are conditioned to buy the traditional flies with split wings, will instinctively feel that they won't catch fish, and the people won't, therefore, buy them. It will take a long time to change something like that. In fact, for a long time to come most people will probably continue to look at the mayfly with its wings together and buy flies with the wings spread.

When the spent-wing spinner is floating on the water it is easy for the trout to take. The fish have no fear that the spinner fly will escape as the dun or any other living insect might. The rises to the spent-wing fly are quiet, deliberate and businesslike. If there is a mixture of different flies on the water with spent wings among

From top to bottom: natural mayfly dun from the front, natural from the side, the usual style of split wings, a better style of wing imitation using a single wing.

them, and the rises are splashy, the trout are taking other insects. If the trout are gently dimpling, they are taking the spinners or some other insect that can't fly away.

The adult mayfly's life span is usually three days. It takes a year, normally, for the immature stage of the mayfly to take place, from the egg laying through the nymph form. Mayfly nymphs vary in shape and size, but most of them are distinguishable by having three tails. Stoneflies, the other common nymphs found in trout streams, have only two tails. As well as varying in shape and size, the mayfly nymphs also vary in coloration, and if the angler wants to make a study of them he might consult one of the specialized books that contain information on nymphs, such as *Nymphs* and *Matching the Hatch* by Ernie Schwiebert, *The Streamside Guide* by Art Flick, *Selective Trout* by Doug Swisher and Carl Richards or *Hatches* by Al Caucci and Bob Nastasi.

The stonefly is a longish fly, and it is readily identifiable by two pairs of wings that lie flat along the back, like sheets of paper on a desk, when the fly is at rest. Bucktail fibers tied flat along the top of the hook shank over the body can imitate a stonefly's wings fairly well. A pair of matched, long, narrow feathers can also do it, as can long, slim, soft, hackle fibers. Stonefly imitations can also have wings cut from translucent material very similar to the real insect's wings, but this material hasn't been generally accepted. Fly-tying is a mixture of exactness, simulation and the limitations of materials, and it's worth mentioning again that most effective flies are not exact imitations, and those that are designed to be exact don't catch many fish unless they are soft and have self movement.

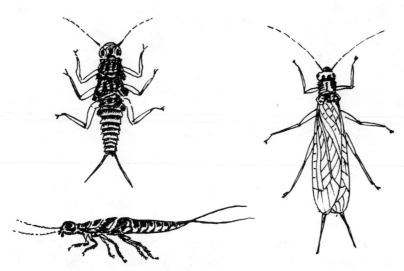

Left, stonefly nymphs; *right,* stonefly adult.

From top to bottom: stonefly from the front, stonefly from above, usual style of wing imitation, a better style of wing imitation.

    The stonefly nymph has two tails, as mentioned before, and has a flat rather than round body. It has three legs standing out conspicuously on each side. The stonefly lives as a nymph for a period of one to three years, depending on the species, and when it is time to hatch it crawls to the streambank and climbs out of the water to do so.

    The caddisfly has two wings that lie over its back in a tentlike shape when the insect is at rest. The wings are longer than the body. The caddisfly wings can be imitated by bucktail fibers tied along the back or by paired, feather wings that follow the tent shape over the back.

The caddisfly doesn't have a nymph stage as do the mayfly and stonefly. It has a larval stage in which it looks like a worm, and most caddisflies build a "house" or case around themselves in this stage for protection. This case may be of grains of sand, bits of wood or other material. The caddis larva in its case, like a turtle safe within its protective shell, lets only its head and legs come out of the front of the case to crawl around and find food. But it is

From top to bottom: caddisfly from the front, caddis from the side, usual style of wing imitation, a better style of wing imitation.

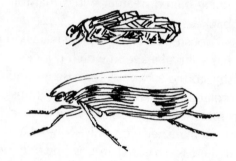

Top, a caddisfly larva in its case; *bottom,* an adult caddisfly.

not always safe in its protective case—I've found the remains of
many a caddis case in the stomachs of trout back in the days when
I used to keep my catches to eat.

When the caddis larva is ready to metamorphose, it spends
some time in a pupal form from which most species swim quickly
to the surface to emerge as winged adults. More information on
caddisflies may be found in *The Caddis and the Angler* by Larry
Solomon and Eric Leiser.

The final insect we are going to consider that hatches into a
winged adult after immature underwater stages is the midge. If
you hold a fine mesh net in the stream you will catch the midges,
and you'll have a chance to see their size, shape and color. They
are almost always on the water year-round in some form. They
are the hardest flies to imitate, calling for the smallest hooks and
the finest leaders as well as considerable skill on the part of the fly
tier and the angler.

Many midges look like miniature houseflies, and the
problem of imitating them lies in getting a body of the right shape
and size on a hook that is not too heavy to be floated or held in the
surface film by the fine hackles or wing materials. When on the
water, these flies are almost impossible to see at any distance, and
the angler often has to guess where his fly is and strike when there
is a rise in that area.

The midge, like the caddisfly, has a larval and pupal stage and no nymph stage. Sometimes the trout will feed on the pupa near the surface, and while the adult imitation will do, it must be fished a little under the surface.

Because of the strength limitations of the very fine thread that must be used for tying midges, and because of the difficulty of tying on tiny hackles and wings for these miniature flies, most of the midge patterns are made very simply. Few are tied as precisely as the larger flies.

Many of the insects on which trout feed do not live in the stream or water at any stage of their lives. These are the terrestrials, the land-based insects that may blunder onto or into the water by accident. There are many and varied forms of terrestrials, ranging from grasshoppers to hornets to ants to angleworms. The fish are familiar with some of the terrestrials. Others an

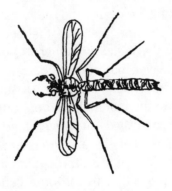

Top, midge adult; *bottom,* midge pupa.

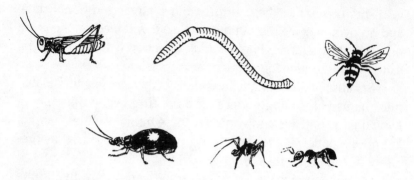

Common terrestrials. *Top row from left to right:* grasshopper, worm, hornet. *Bottom row from left to right:* beetle, spider, ant.

individual trout may never have seen, but that doesn't mean it won't take them, sometimes without hesitation. For example, it is almost as if by instinct that a fish takes a cicada. The cicada is an insect with a long life cycle, and there will be more years than a trout's normal lifetime between their years of hatching. This instinct to take the cicada whether it moves or not is like the ability of the beaver that builds a dam when the materials and opportunity are given to it, even when for many generations it has been deprived of the materials and opportunity. Trout that have been fished for intensively, however, tend to be more cautious, and they are more likely to take a grasshopper in areas in which grasshoppers abound, for example, than an unfamiliar insect.

The main terrestrials to use on a certain stream, then, are those that are common in the area. Grasshoppers, ants, small inchworms and other bugs that fall to the water from the over-hanging trees and grasses, and angleworms that are washed into the stream by heavy runoff are all anticipated, recognized and accepted as normal fare. Only when a fish has no hunger or when there is something suspect about a terrestrial imitation will it refuse it.

A profusion of terrestrials coming down the stream can sometimes be even more confusing than a difficult hatch. There may be some insects hatching out and trout rising furiously but refusing to take any of the hatching aquatic insects. A close study in such a case might reveal that tiny, green inchworms are dropping to the water from the branches that overhang the stream. It might show tiny black beetles that drift like icebergs, ninety-nine percent submerged and almost invisible from above. It may show flying ants that drift without motion like spent-wing mayflies.

Often the appearance of certain terrestrials is local in nature. This calls for stream study by the angler who doesn't have the advantage of local knowledge or advice. But whenever you overhear someone say, "About this time of year we have a bunch of little, yellow caterpillars falling from the trees, and when we do, the trout feed on them" try to find out more about what they look like, and try to find out which imitations local anglers use.

Trout that are feeding have a tendency to be selective and to concentrate on a particular type of food that's available at the moment. It's like a man who says to himself, "It's blueberry time, and I'm going to pick and eat blueberries until I've finally had my fill. There may be some raspberries and blackberries scattered among the blueberries, but I don't want to be bothered by the seeds. I can eat them later, perhaps, when I'm hungry again and the blueberries are gone." It is important for the angler to have a basic understanding of trout-stream insects if he is going to be successful: It helps him to understand what the fish are feeding on, how that thing behaves and what it looks like.

The great modern interest by many anglers in stream life is a fine thing for angling. It gives a greater depth to the sport, and it is more and more necessary because fish are becoming increasingly more sophisticated and selective with the increasing fishing pressure. The modern angler has become quite scientific in his approach, and he often learns the Latin names of the insects and has an understanding of them that few of us old-timers ever tried to attain.

I'm of the old school, and, by considering all of the insects as *bugs* and knowing about the general types of insects such as the mayflies, stoneflies, caddisflies, midges and terrestrials, I have been able to fish very successfully. I am still not well educated in entomology. I don't know the Latin names of the bugs, but I figure the trout don't know the Latin names either. Nor do they know the names of the fly patterns I fish with, and I, too, care very little about their names. I tend to pattern my flies after what I know of the insects in the area rather than after the strict patterns that appear in the books, magazines and catalogs.

Knowing the Latin names will not impress the fish or make you a better fisherman. The scientific Latin names do what they are designed to do: identify an insect so that you can talk to someone about it. As an artist I can make a sketch that will identify any bug I want to talk about, and that has been a great help in some intense lunch-table conversations on flies and techniques.

As exciting and intriguing as matching the hatch may be, breaking through the hatch with something far removed from it can also be exciting. An angler should have in his mind certain fly patterns that he believes some trout will be partial to, no matter what the water and fly-hatch conditions are. At first he will probably have to take someone else's advice on what patterns these flies may be, but as he fishes and develops his own favorites, those will be the ones he will use when the going is tough.

Unfortunately, when most people are trying to match the hatch, they get close to it but not close enough for success. Let's assume there is a hatch of Pale Watery Duns that are about the size of a #20 fly, but the angler doesn't have anything smaller than a #16. He does have a fair variety of #16 patterns, and he keeps trying them one after another to catch some of the rising trout. But he is unsuccessful.

The problem here is that the angler is close, but not close enough. He ends up with complete failure and becomes more determined to be able to match the hatch the next time. But the next time he hits a small hatch, it is still smaller than the #18s and #20s he has added to his fly box. And if they are not too large, they are the wrong shape or color. Again he is frustrated.

If he had definitely moved out of the hatch size and shape into other, larger patterns, he would have had a very good chance of success. The trout that turns down a #16 because it is not a #18 will not look at a #12 Royal Wulff, for example, with the same critical eye. The fish knows it is not a fake version of what it has been taking, but something else completely and maybe something it likes. In order to intrigue a selectively feeding trout with something else you have to go to other, larger or very different flies. This is what I call my strawberries-and-cream theory.

I love fresh strawberries, especially when the cream on them is whipped, thick and real. When the local strawberries get ripe and show up in the local stores, or the "pick-your-own" signs go up, it is a memorable time for me. The northern growing season now extends into fall with late-bearing plants, and that's been great; but there are months when we're snowbound, and there are no strawberries in the markets.

Sometimes, though, a restaurant will have fresh strawberries on the menu in January, and when one does, and I come along, it has a customer. Trout, like people, have minds and special preferences of their own. "A fish is a fish is a fish" isn't quite true. Fish

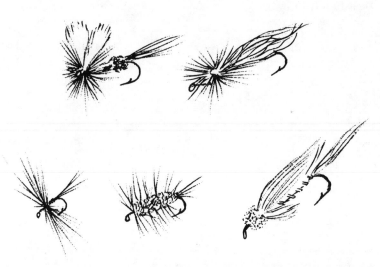

Strawberries-and-cream flies. *Top row from left to right:* Royal Wulff, Surface Stonefly. *Bottom row:* Spider, Woolly Worm, Muddler Minnow.

can differ widely. Some are conformists, some are not. Some jump excitedly when hooked, some jump listlessly or not at all.

I feel that trout have certain preferences that they never lose, and when a particular type of food comes along they will go out of their way to get it even though they are feeding at the time on other food that is plentiful. When I float a big stonefly imitation, a Royal Wulff or a grasshopper imitation over a fish that's regularly feeding on the hatch of the day, I know I can often expect to get a rise. Some special flies affect trout like strawberries and cream affect me, even when they are unexpected and out of season.

Among the flies that I find particularly useful in this situation are the Royal Wulff, Surface Stonefly (which I describe under "Special Flies"), Spider, Skater, a big stonefly nymph, Woolly Worm, a streamer and a Muddler.

For the last few years, when confronted with a hatch situation, I first try to match the hatch and usually succeed to some degree. Then I break away from the hatch entirely, and, covering more water and not restricting myself to rising fish, I have found that when I strike a difficult hatch I am likely to catch as many fish per hour with my strawberries-and-cream flies as I did with my best hatch imitations.

FOUR

A Basic Assortment of Trout Flies

Each fly is a dream we cast out to fool fish. Those flies in which we have the most faith we fish with more hope, more determination and for longer periods. Because we give these flies the best chance they are the ones that catch most of the fish for us. The flies we are doubtful about we only tie on when conditions are poorest and our favorite flies have already failed. We don't really give these doubtfuls a fair chance, and if we put them on during the best fishing times instead of our favorites, we might change our views of which flies are best.

I feel that trout flies can be divided into two types: naturals and attractors. The naturals try to imitate as closely as possible the preferred foods of trout. The attractors tend to have flash and color and are designed to intrigue the trout, appealing to its curiosity. To put together a basic assortment of trout flies, my advice is to include at least one of each type in the following basic categories: dry flies, wet flies, streamers, nymphs and terrestrials. There are also a couple of special flies that should be included.

For the natural dry fly, I'd choose the Adams. It looks like an imitation of so many natural insects that I feel it's invaluable. The Adams is mottled, has semi-translucent wings and a body of medium color density. I believe it is the buggiest-looking dry fly of all; however, if you know of one that is buggier-looking, then that should be your choice.

My first choice for an attractor dry fly is the Royal Wulff. I think it is the most exciting-looking dry fly. While as an imitation of an insect it is not beyond the realm of possibility, it is on the edge of it. Again, if there's a fly you feel is more exciting than this one, then that should be your first choice for an attractor dry fly.

I'll take the Gold-Ribbed Hare's Ear for my natural wet fly because it is the most buggy that I know of. It has a good neutral coloration and a tiny bit of flash imparted by the tinsel ribbing. If the wings are too long and extend beyond the body of the fly, I

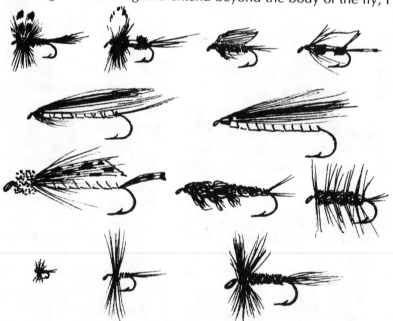

Basic assortment of trout flies. *Top row from left to right:* Adams, Royal Wulff, Gold-Ribbed Hare's Ear wet fly, Royal Coachman wet fly. *Second row:* Black-Nosed Dace, Mickey Finn. *Third row:* Muddler Minnow, Stonefly nymph, Woolly Worm. *Bottom row:* midge, Spider, Gray Wulff.

simply trim them back to a length just shorter than the body with my scissors. I have found that wet flies often have wings too long for my taste, and when I trim them off I try to make the edge ragged to look natural to the fish, and so the fibers of the wing make a little more motion as it's fished.

I find it hard to pick a favorite among the wet-fly attractors, but I'll choose the Royal Coachman because of its flashy coloration. On some waters other flashy wets are most successful, such as the Silver Doctor and the Alexandra, and there is something to be said for the stark, light-and-dark contrast of the Black Gnat. However, for an all-around attractor wet fly, I'll stick with the Royal Coachman.

In choosing a natural streamer I look for a pronounced lateral stripe in the pattern, because so many fish have either a dark or a flashy stripe along the side. A Black-Nosed Dace is my choice for a natural streamer. For the attractor, I feel it's hard to beat the Mickey Finn; it has both color and flash. It works well both on the sophisticated trout of the wild rivers and the smart old browns of our hard-fished streams.

There is a special category of streamers that is important, and it's the Muddler. I wouldn't want to be without this type of fly. The standard Muddler Minnow is fine, but almost any combination of tinsel and materials behind a Muddler head, within reason, should work well. The Surface Stonefly fished as a streamer could well fit the same category.

For the natural nymph I'd choose a fuzzy stonefly imitation. I think it's the most buggy looking—for the trout and myself. Stoneflies, like mayflies and caddisflies, are fairly universal in our trout streams, and because of the stonefly nymph mult-year aquatic stage, they are large when the mayflies and caddisflies are almost all eggs or very small nymphs. When you're not trying to match a specific hatch I feel the bigger the mouthful offered, within reason, the farther away a fish can spot it and the more worthwhile it will seem to the fish to strike it.

For my attractor nymph I'll choose a Woolly Worm. I like olive-green ones and black ones best. It doesn't seem to me to look much like anything a trout should expect to see in a stream, but it is close enough in appearance to so many caterpillars and nymphs that it works well. The palmer-tied hackle fibers give the Woolly Worm a fine sense of internal movement in the water.

For terrestrial imitations there is nothing like the grasshopper imitation in the right time of year and right waters, but for all-around use, my natural-terrestrial choice is the Gray Wulff. It looks like many land bugs when tied with a fairly heavy body and a medium amount of hackle to provide flotation. For a flashy terrestrial I'll take the Royal Wulff in the larger sizes—#8 or #10. Another fly to remember as an attractor terrestrial is the little, floating bug that is designed for sunfish; this bug is a very good trout producer when the time is right.

There is one other fly that I would not like to be without and that is the Spider, in #16, olive, grizzly or badger. It can be turned into a Skater by using a fine leader and a greased line.

Actually no list of flies as short as this one will fill the bill for any but the casual fly fisherman. For more serious anglers, these are flies not to be left out of larger selections. The fly to use depends so much on the water to be fished that if I fished one area more than others I would extend my selection to cover those waters I fished most. Still, with the basic assortment described here, I would feel capable of doing a fairly good job anywhere on this continent.

There is also one basic tool that I would not like to be without on a trout stream. That is a pair of scissors. If you take a fly with fluffy hackle, such as a Spider or Bivisible, there are many ways to trim the shape to make a more effective pattern for that particular moment.

The Spider especially is a fly that I have long been trimming. It is one of my ace-in-the-hole flies. When a small fly is hatching and trout are taking it with occasional rises, I often put on a #16, #18 or even a #20 Spider. On some occasions, as on Montana's Red Rock River in 1977, I started fishing to occasional risers with a #18 Spider. In a few minutes I fooled one of the trout and caught him. When none of the other fish would take the fly I cut off all of the hackles on the lower half of the fly. With the fly floating at

Scissor-clipped Spider.

hook level on the water's surface with only the bushy fibers in the air, I caught another fish. Then no action. Scissors again. I cut off all the top fibers, leaving only three or four fibers coming out horizontally from each side of the fly. Now the fly was floating like a spent-wing pattern, with very long and practically invisible wings, and I caught another trout. The spent-wing version drew another rise that I missed. Then again no more action. I cut off all of the remaining hackles and ended up with nothing but the thread wrapping and a lot of very short fibers sticking out near the head of the fly for about $1/32$ of an inch. That fly was a pretty fair representation of a tiny nymph, and I took two more fish with it. Finally, I put that fly in my "very small nymph" box for possible use at another time.

Spiders are one of the easiest flies to tie, and I describe how to do so under "Spiders and Skaters." If you tie your own flies you may be able to turn Spiders out at a rate of as many as thirty an hour, so they're a good fly to cut up on stream while experimenting. Bivisibles, too, are easy flies to tie, and good ones to trim while on the stream. That ball of fluff can be trimmed to almost any conceivable shape. With the scissors, you can trim a Bivisible into a shape like that of a bee, a wasp, a spent-wing or a caterpillar. The greatest fun of having and using flies is to innovate with them when the ordinary or favorite patterns don't work. Whether or not you tie your own, trimming flies can be an intriguing part of fly-fishing.

Modifying a fly with a pair of scissors can only take a fly in one direction: smaller. Cutting away some hackle will make a fly float lower on the surface. Cutting away wings can change the character of a dry fly, making it look more like an emerging insect than one that has already hatched. Careful trimming of a dry fly on top and bottom can make it into a spent-wing pattern. The artful use of scissors on the stream can spell the difference between catching fish and failing to catch fish.

It is time that anglers realize that fly patterns aren't sacred and can be altered to better effect. The art of fly-tying has always dictated that the ends of any hackle or feather fiber on a fly should be natural and not trimmed. The soft, fine ends where the fiber fades away into nothing give more life when fished than the same fiber trimmed off to leave a stiff, blunt end. These carefully matched ends move more softly in the water, and they spread more smoothly on the surface. I still tie flies with care to match the natural fiber ends, and I eliminate each cut fiber or broken fiber while tying. But, on the stream, where it really counts, I've changed my habits a bit and will do there what I never do at the tying table. Actually, if you stop to think about it, the parts of an insect that hackle fibers imitate, such as legs, don't taper off to a fine point as the untrimmed fibers do, but have blunt ends as cut fibers do.

Another tool that can help the angler change the character or look of his fly is the Magic Marker pen, or another of the waterproof marking pens. I first used one to change the tone and color of small flies when trying to fool some very wise fish in Armstrong's Spring Creek in Montana. This was in 1964, and we were making a film for a CBS "Sports Spectacular" show. A lot was riding on our ability to catch fish for the cameras. With the Magic Marker, a Pale Watery Dun became something darker, something the trout liked better.

Changing color or shade can be very effective at times. It is better, of course, to carry a full complement of flies with a wide variety of color and shade in your vest than to make up for a lack of the proper fly with streamside coloring. Just as scissors can only make a fly smaller, the Magic Marker can only make light-colored flies brighter or darker. If you must limit your flies to only a few, then include a number of light-colored ones and carry some marking pens.

Whether you are sitting at a tying table making a basic selection of flies to help cover your needs, or ordering them from a catalog, it is important to know which basic types of flies should be included. It is also very important for you to remember that tools such as scissors or the marking pen can actually broaden your fly selection very easily. The best-equipped angler is not necessarily the one with the most expensive and extensive array of flies; usually he is the one equipped with the foresight to carry the basic patterns and the ingenuity to alter his flies into something the fish will want to strike.

FIVE

The Wulff Flies

I have a letter somewhere in my files from Ken Lockwood, a fine fisherman and outdoor writer from New Jersey. He wrote me soon after Ray Bergman's *Trout* came out in 1938 and brought the Wulff flies to the notice of fishermen. Ken explained that he'd come up with a version of the Gray Wulff that had a clipped-deerhair body instead of the angora-wool body. It was being called the Irresistible. Did I mind? I wrote back to wish him well and say that I didn't mind.

Trout fishermen don't seem ready for categories of flies; instead they seem to stick by particular patterns. The Wulff flies, like Don Gapen's original Muddler Minnow, should be only the beginning—opening up new categories, systems, or fields of flies for the trout fisherman. The clipped-deerhair fly head was the new and especially effective *idea* introduced by the Muddler; it should be tied not only with a tinsel body and turkey-feather

The Irresistible.

wings, but in every conceivable combination of materials that make up flies. Similarly, the Gray Wulff was only the first fly in a new category for the fisherman.

Those first days and weeks of trying out the Wulff flies were a dream. I put on a Gray Wulff while fishing the Salmon River near Malone, New York, with Dan Bailey, and I caught fifty-one trout with the same fly without once having to take it from the leader, which was a fantastic feat at the time. I used Mucilin line grease as a fly floatant instead of the universally used mixture of paraffin dissolved in benzine or gasoline, into which the fly was dipped. I found I could catch five or six trout between greasings, and I was glad I had secured the fly so well with lacquer when I tied it. Anything that makes fishing simpler and lets me spend more time with my fly on the water and less time in fussing with things to get ready or while on the stream makes me happier.

I used many kinds of hairs for the tails and wings of these flies. I even bought some "Chinese" bucktails that were small and the color of red fox fur and used the material for the Wulff flies. It worked very well. I tried other hairs (I failed to try calftail back in the early days of testing), and decided that bucktail gave the best flotation and durability to the flies. Calftail, while it does not have quite the elegance of bucktail, has great floating properties, and it is a lot easier to match into proper wing lengths and work into proper spreads, or positioning of the wings.

My original instincts had been right. I had felt that a heavy-bodied, large fly—I used flies tied on #10 hooks mostly—would be more attractive to the trout than the slim-bodied, small patterns of the day. The trout would be able to see it from a greater depth, and it would seem to them like a bigger mouthful and something that was worth coming up for. It might even look at a quick glance like some strange terrestrial: a bee, a wasp or a fluttering moth. Part of my deep feeling was that if it looked like a bug—if it had a familiar look to the trout—whether identical to the mayfly or not, it would draw rises.

Soon after the Wulff flies began to gain popularity, Dan Bailey started to go to Montana in the summers to fish. Because he taught science at Brooklyn Polytechnical Institute for a living, Dan had his summers free to fish. Preston Jennings, a great student of stream insects, was writing a book about insects and trout flies. Dan showed him the Wulff flies when they fished together in Montana, saying he was tying a lot of them to sell and was catching a lot of fish on them. Preston looked at them and said they imitated no insects, and he couldn't believe that they were actually good trout flies. Although the Montana fishing convinced Preston that they would take fish, he didn't put them in his well-known *A Book of Trout Flies,* published in 1935. He told me he couldn't figure out why trout liked them so well. It was, he said, one of the unreasonable things about trout fishing.

To tie the Wulff, begin the thread near the hook eye, wind down the shank to the bend, and return back up the shank to the start. At this point, lacquer may be applied to give a good bond between the thread and hook shank, which will prevent the twisting of thread and materials as the fly is tied. Select bucktail to be used for the tail, and match the fine ends of the hair so they are

The Gray Wulff at the right looks much buggier than the typical dry fly of 1930 and earlier.

as even as possible. This can be done by pulling out the longer hairs and resetting them so they are even with the tips of the others, or by placing the hairs in a narrow container, such as a cartridge shell, and tapping the container gently on the tabletop.

Place the tail along the hook shank with the tips extending beyond the bend of the hook to the length illustrated. Wrap the thread down to the bend of the hook, and clip off the excess hair near the eye of the hook. Apply a drop of lacquer to the thread wraps along the hook shank; the lacquer will penetrate to the hook and also remain on the thread to help set the angora-wool body tightly when it is applied in the next step. Good setting of the body makes for long life in a fly.

Tie in a length of angora wool at the head and wrap the thread to the bend and back to the head. Wrap the angora wool forward, forming the proper shape of body, as shown in the illustrations, and tie it off at the head. As you are winding the angora, also rotate the material to avoid twisting it, forming a smooth body.

Select the bucktail to be used for the wings and even the tips in the same manner that you evened the tips of the bucktail used for the tail. (If calftail is used for the wings, the evening process is not necessary.) Lay the bucktail over the shank, with the tips facing forward over the hook eye as shown. Tie the hair in, then bring the thread in front of the wings and make them stand up vertically by building up a wall of thread in front of the bucktail. By splitting the hair into two wings and winding between and around them at the base, the wings are set into the right position. A drop or two of lacquer should be applied between the wings at their base. The lacquer will penetrate the hair and thread and set the wings securely to the hook. The lacquer should still be soft as the hackles are wound, which will set the hackle fibers securely in place. Saddle hackles, which I perfer, are usually strong of fiber but without great strength where the fibers join the hackle stem. Setting their bases in lacquer makes a much more durable fly.

Two long saddle hackles are used for the standard Wulff. After you tie them in, bring the first one back between the wings

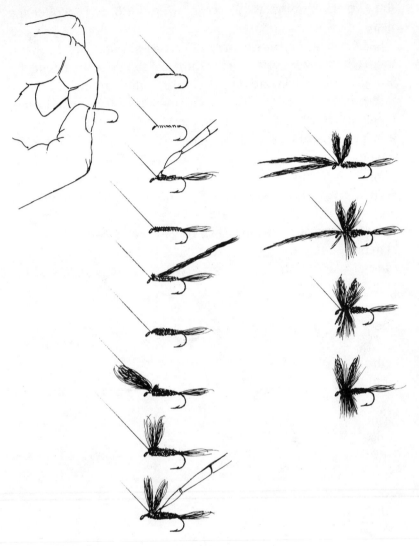

Tying the Wulff.

and wind it around the shank close behind the wings until it is just long enough to pass between the two upright wings again. Bring it between the wings and hold it at the hook eye between your forefinger and thumb. Wind the second hackle around the shank in front of the wings to the hackle's tip. Wrap the tying thread over the two hackle tips, trim excess, whip-finish and lacquer the head.

Of course there are many versions of the Wulff flies. I've seen them with the wings slanted forward, and I've seen them with the wings slanted backward. I've even read a short article in a minor publication, by a man I've never met or corresponded with, entitled, "The Right Way to Tie the Wulff Flies." But all this is good, because the Wulff fly is a category of flies, not an inflexible pattern.

I tie the Wulff flies in a variety of patterns. On #12, #14 or #16 hooks, with slimmer-than-usual bodies and wings, and with less winds of hackle, I use them to imitate the hendricksons when those flies are on the water. On a very long-shanked hook, with a slim body and long tail, the Wulff fly looks like a small dragonfly. On very large and heavy hooks, when the hackles aren't big

Top row from left to right: Wulff with wings slanted forward, Wulff tied with a slim body to imitate a mayfly, spent-wing Wulff. *Middle row:* Wulff tied on long-shanked hook to imitate a damselfly, standard Wulff, Scraggly. *Bottom row:* Wulff with clipped-hair body, Wulff with wings slanted back, single-wing Wulff.

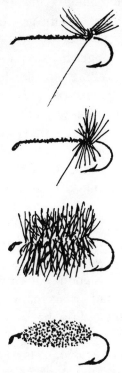

To put on a clipped-deerhair body, apply the deerhair in small bunches and bind with thread to flare. Continue to apply the bunches until the desired body length is reached. Then shape the ends with scissors.

enough or strong enough to give proper flotation, I use Ken Lockwood's idea and tie a clipped-deerhair body to float the big fly.

One of my variations is the Scraggly. It floats even higher than the standard Wulff, and it has a bulkier body. It is, perhaps, a better imitation of a nondescript, flying terrestrial than the standard Wulff.

The Scraggly is tied by using chenille or another bulky body material and winding a hackle palmer style down the body. The body and hackle add bulk and flotation at the same time. The Grizzly Scraggly is a Gray Wulff with a grizzly hackle wound over a chenille body; the Bumble Bee Scraggly is a Gray Wulff that has a chenille body of alternating yellow and black with a badger hackle wound over it to replace the gray body of the Gray Wulff; the White Moth Scraggly is a White Wulff that has a cream chenille body with a badger hackle palmer tied over it. These Scragglies float high and attract attention from hungry fish deep in the water because of the size of their bodies.

I use Wulff flies for bass as well as for trout and salmon. In #4 or larger they have considerable bulk and will attract bass, yet they are lighter to cast than the average-size bass bugs. Heavily hackled with a clipped-deerhair body, they can be jumped across the surface a bit from time to time to make them even more attractive to the bass.

Of course, as I was originally dealing with a mayfly imitation, I tried out a single wing as well as the split wings. I made up a few dozen flies with a wing that consisted of a single tuft of bucktail, either vertical or slanting back at an angle like a mayfly's wings. It seemed that I had just as many rises to the single-wing versions as I did to the split-wing versions. I was especially successful with the single-wing Royal Wulff. But since I was poor at the time, as was almost everyone else during those Depression days, I tied and promoted the Wulff flies the way my customers wanted them—with split wings. But, while I feel that single-wing flies are better imitations than are split wings, divided wings do give better flotation and are more visible to the angler. And the illusion the split-wing Wulffs create seems completely adequate.

When fishing fast water I like Wulff flies with quite bushy wings and sometimes as many as three hackles. They should be tied in this manner so they ride high and don't drown in the rough water. In very still water, I use either the bushy flies as terrestrial imitations or the more sparsely tied patterns as imitations of stream insects. I tie almost all of my flies in a wide variety of density of materials as well as in a wide variety of colors. My use of hackle may vary from the normally bushy to none at all, such as in a spinner pattern when the wings are spread out horizontally to imitate the mayfly's spent wings.

When tying spent-wing Wulffs with no hackle, I use the fine

hairs from the tip end of the bucktail, and I flare these hairs out at the wings and at the tail to give maximum flotation with minimum visibility. These tip-end bucktail hairs are more wiry, and they have very fine diameters. They are stronger than the rest of the hairs on the bucktail. In this instance the bucktail is far superior to calftail. The color may be varied by dyeing, and the bodies may be tied thick or thin, depending upon the spinner being imitated. Most spinners have more slender bodies than the standard Wulff flies.

The Wulff flies will also serve as bulky, substitute Skaters when tied with the usual or a greater amount of hackle support and wing thickness. In 1933, a salmon fisherman on the Liscombe River in Nova Scotia, to whom I'd given a Wulff to try, reported good luck with it. I came to watch him fish because he was doing better than we were on the Ecum Secum River. I found him fishing the gift fly as a wet fly, dragging it across the surface of the pool below a fall. I hadn't explained to him when I gave him the fly how dry flies were fished, and apparently he had never fished with dry flies before. By fishing it just as he would a wet fly, he made it into a substitute Skater.

I tried the fly with a free float, and I failed to get a rise. It may have been because he'd caught all the takers with his dragging fly, or because the salmon actually liked the dragged fly better than the free-floating fly. I don't know, because he had no rises while we both fished the pool. This is typical of the situations that leave you to wonder forever about the reasons salmon take a fly.

Although I tend to fish my dry flies, except for Skaters, in a dead drift with the current, I do use motion, or change to fishing under the surface, when I know where a fish lies and the dead drift doesn't interest it. By the slightest twitch of the rod the fly can be moved just enough to suggest life. Sometimes, when the fly is floating and the leader is underwater, I quickly jerk the fly under the surface just as it comes to the fish. Then I let it continue an underwater dead drift. Both trout and salmon have taken the fly after this maneuver often enough to keep me trying it on difficult fish.

When a fly pops under water just above a salmon, and it decides to take it, it has to make a quick turn to come up under it. In executing the turn, it makes a big boil and often pokes its nose up out of the water in the taking surge. I have many memories of fine salmon that were taken when a big White Wulff was suddenly submerged. This tactic works better when using big flies for salmon than it does with the smaller flies used for trout.

A strong case against using motion with dry flies is that when the fly is moved so is the leader and line. Any smart trout, seeing the motion of the fly and at the same time the motion of the leader, will put two and two together and realize that the fly is not an insect but something attached to something else and, therefore, suspect. Motion should always be used with care, and almost never with smart fish. Skaters are the exception, and they call for very long, fine leaders and motion of a type that will put the fish's mind on the fly with total disregard of the leader.

The many techniques used to fish the Wulff flies and the many different insects the Wulff flies may imitate reflect that the flies are a category of patterns. The Wulff flies almost seem made to be tied in various patterns. I like to think of flies such as the Wulff as categories, in the same manner as trout and salmon form a category with the first name of *Salmo*.

S I X

Spiders and Skaters

Although I had used Spiders for trout in the Catskills and Adirondacks earlier, my first real proof of their special effectiveness
came in 1933 when I was camping beside the Ecum Secum River
in Nova Scotia. It was a hot, dry summer, and the river was very
low; fishing for both trout and salmon was hard. The run of sea
trout was in the river, but few were being caught, and none were
caught, ever, in the mornings before the daily sea breeze came
up, when the pools were like glass.

Defying local tradition, I went out to fish for trout in the
morning. Having studied the smooth pools, I had seen small
dimples in the surface. I started fishing with a #16 Spider, the
smallest fly I had, and I caught trout immediately. The trout were
sea-run eastern brook trout, and they ranged from one to over four
pounds—it was wonderful fishing. Most of the trout were silvery

63

on the sides and belly and dark green on the back: the brook trout's sea coloration. They were bright fish, and only a few had started the change that would, in less than a month, give them the coloration of a native brook trout in its stream.

After I had caught many fish, the local fishermen came out to take their share. It was easy to see why they had said the fish couldn't be caught when there wasn't a breeze blowing. It took a breeze to camouflage the heavy leaders and large flies they used. The flies were typical of those days: the different Coachmen patterns, the Cowdung, the Black Gnat and others—all wet flies on #12 and larger hooks. Even if they had used dry flies larger than the #16 Spider I used, and tied them to finer leaders, I believe the fishermen would have caught some fish on those smooth, early-morning pools.

I caught a lot of trout and gave them away to the people who owned the land we were camping on and to other people who had befriended us in some way, keeping only those that we needed for our own use. In the Depression food was as scarce as money; I remember that a cow was killed and butchered in the village, and it sold for fifteen cents a pound, any cut. There were more people who wanted fish than there were fish to give away, and we knew only a few of the villagers.

I remember walking along the highway one evening, after a trip to the shore, and a woman called out to me from across the road: "You just wait til it comes a rain and river comes up and you won't be catching all those fish on your little tiny flies!" I found out later that this woman was Dan MacIntosh's wife. Dan was one of the local fishermen, and a good one, but he hadn't been able to catch fish with his usual gear. When I gave him a few Spiders to try out, he straightened them out or lost them in the few fish that rose to them. When I came alongside his boat to give him a few more flies, I noticed the leader to which he'd tied his remaining Spider. It was heavy, coiled like a spring, and the fly at the leader's end looked like a tiny knot at the end of a rope. I had given him some fine gut leader tippets to go with the original flies—nylon was still far in the future—and he'd broken them off,

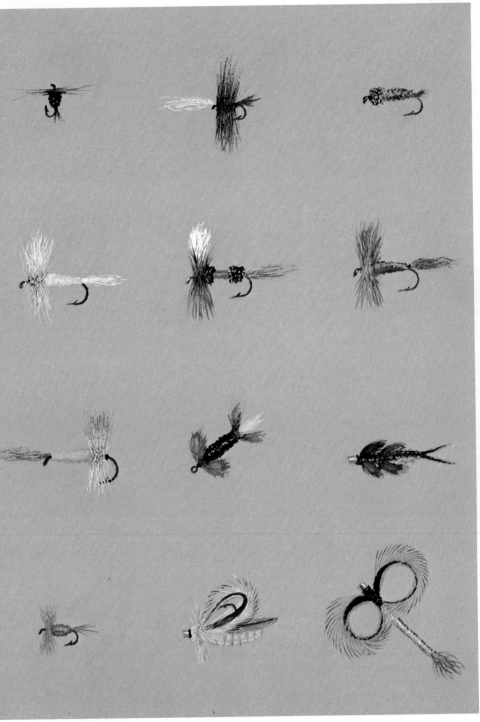

Left to right, top to bottom: Fat-Bodied Spider, Prefontaine, Gray Nymph, White Wulff, Royal Wulff, Gray Wulff, Olive Wulff (backwards), Wretched Mess, Stonefly Nymph, Coty Stillwater, Flexible Hopper, Green Damsel (looped hackle and flexible)

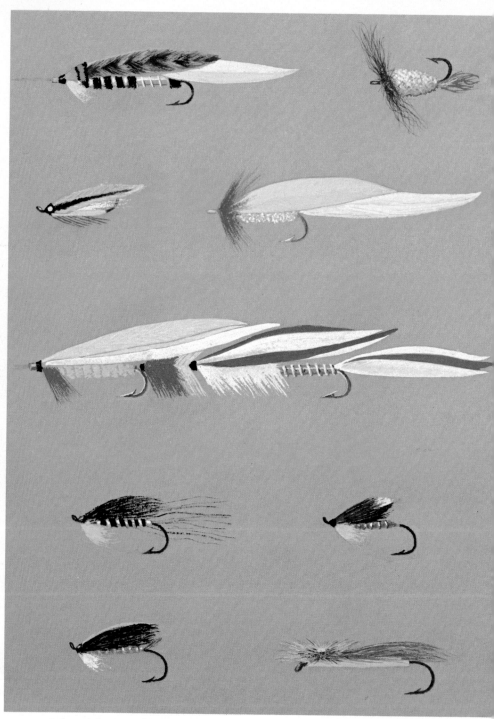

Left to right, top to bottom: **Perfect Streamer (flexible), Skidder, Weedless Wonder, Kulik Killer, Sea Wulff, Haggis, Lady Joan, Cullman's Choice, Surface Stonefly**

losing both fish and fly, when he tried to lift the fish right into the boat by the leader. He discarded the fine tippets as too weak.

It turned out that I was the only one who could catch fish under those difficult fishing conditions on the Ecum Secum, and I had to stop giving away the fine tippets and small flies because I was running out of them. I continued to catch fish and to give them away as fairly as I could. My supply of small hooks dwindled to about three, and I remember catching trout on a bare #16 hook, fished as a nymph, after all the materials had come off. I explained this to one of the locals by telling him that fish didn't know steel from grass and couldn't know that it was the hook that hurt them instead of the feathers until the fish had a real chance to be educated to the hook itself by being hooked and getting away a few times.

But it was the Spider fly and its special effectiveness on the low water of the Ecum Secum that taught me *my* lesson. Since those days I have never underestimated the capabilities of the Spider.

The Spider is an easy fly to tie; basically it is only a hackle wound over a thread base. Normally a short-shanked hook is used, but any small dry-fly hook will do. Start the thread at the point where you will begin wrapping the hackle, and tie in the hackle, wrapping the thread down the hook shank to just ahead of the bend. The hackle should be tied in so that it extends beyond the eye of the hook as shown in the illustration. Selection of a hackle with the proper overall length and the proper fiber length is important. You must have the right number of hackle turns on the fly to provide the amount of flotation you want. I tie my Spiders with anywhere from two to ten turns of hackle. After winding the hackle, enough of the hackle tip should remain so that, after being wrapped over with the thread, it will extend beyond the bend of the hook to form the tail. With two turns of hackle the Spider will show very little in the way of a silhouette, and its floating properties will limit its use to smooth-water fishing. A Spider with ten turns of hackle will be very fluffy, and it will float high in fast water and can also be used as a Skater. A true

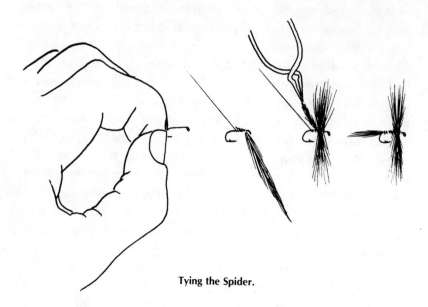

Tying the Spider.

Skater, however, is tied with bucktail and only about two to five turns of hackle, and it will skip over fairly rough water as well as smooth water.

To tie the Skater I seek out the long, fine, wiry hairs of the bucktail. I match them so that the natural tip ends are all just about even. (The method is described in the previous chapter.) I cut the butt ends of the bunch to the proper length which should be determined by the hook size, retaining the proportions shown in the illustrations. I normally tie the Skater on #16 and #18 hooks for trout and in sizes up to #12 for salmon.

The thread should be wrapped on the hook shank to a point near the bend and back to the eye, and a drop of lacquer should be applied to secure it to the hook. The bucktail is tied in, tips extending beyond the hook eye, and it should be spread so that the fibers are evenly distributed around the circumference of the hook shank. Bend the bucktail fibers back, toward the bend of the hook, and build a wall of thread in front of the fibers' base. The wall of thread should hold the fibers so that they stand out from the shank at about a ninety-degree angle when released. Usually I cock the ring of fibers at a slight angle as shown. This ensures that the hook rides point up when the fly is skated. I feel that the fly hooks better in this position.When I have the ring of fibers in the right position, I lock them in place with a drop of lacquer at the base of the fibers so the fly will always skate when pulled across the surface on a greased line and leader. To finish the Skater, I tie two to five turns of hackle behind the bucktail fibers and use the tip of the hackle for the tail, as in the Spider. A white hackle for this rear face and tail increases the fly's visibility.

I created a variation of the Skater pattern while a group of us were fishing the Moisie River, one of the world's finest Atlantic salmon rivers. I named it the Prefontaine after our host, Alain Prefontaine.

During an afternoon discussion the subject of the size of flies for salmon came up, and I mentioned that I had caught a sixteen-pound salmon on a #16 Spider at my camps at Portland Creek,

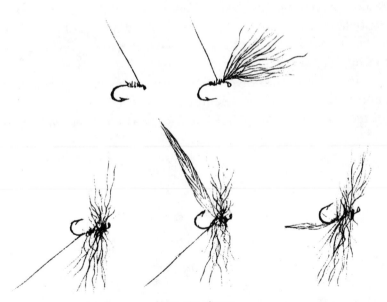

Tying the Skater.

Newfoundland. We decided that a twenty-pound salmon on a #16 single-hook fly would be something that probably hadn't yet been done and would be an historic event. We all decided to try it, and if we succeeded, we would form a club called the Sixteen/Twenty Club.

That afternoon we tested the #16 hooks that we had, and we found that they would either bend or break, depending on whether they were old Alcocks that I had in my fly-tying kit or Mustads of a more recent vintage, when subject to about a four-pound pull. This gave us all a pretty good idea of what a feat it would be to land a twenty-pound or heavier salmon on a #16 hook.

I had some #16 Spiders that I always carried for difficult salmon, but they seemed woefully sparse. To make the fluffiest possible fly for so small a hook, I tied the high-floating, Skaterlike Prefontaine. To give extra floating and skating abilities, this fly had a long bucktail snoot out front, and three full hackles on the shank with the hackle tips combining to form the tail.

When we fished that evening, the five of us were using either Spiders or Prefontaines. I was delighted at the unique action of the Prefontaine when skated. It bounced along on top of the rough water like a Bivisible, but the bucktail snoot made it flop from side to side in an attractive fashion.

The Moisie is known for big fish. Any salmon hooked is almost as likely to be over twenty pounds as under it. To be fishing for these great fish with so small a fly was giving us two chal-

The Prefontaine.

lenges: first, to get a big salmon to rise to such a small fly; second, to capture so tough a fish on so small a hook.

Alain Prefontaine was the only one of the five of us to hook a fish that evening on a #16, and he played it into the darkness before it came within reach of my tailer. When hung on the scales, it brought the needle down to the twenty-and-a-half-pound mark. The Sixteen/Twenty Club had its first member. I had chosen an appropriate name for the fly.

All of this took place in July 1964, and since then only two more of our five have made the club. I made it a few days later with two twenty-four-pounders in the same afternoon, and in ensuing years I have taken over a dozen salmon over twenty pounds on a #16 fly, the largest of which weighed twenty-seven pounds. Lucien Rolland made it three years later with a twenty-one-pounder, after a heartbreaker the second year with a fish that was between nineteen-and-a-half pounds and twenty pounds. In 1977 Lucien caught a second salmon over twenty pounds on a #16 fly.

It was very difficult to get big fish on that small of a fly, and I managed to do it by fishing with nothing else for weeks, except for on a few occasions. Unfortunately, on one of those occasions, when I was fishing with a conventional #6 fly, I hooked and landed a thirty-pounder. I wish I had been using a #16 fly, because I dream of someday catching a salmon of thirty pounds or more on a #16 fly as a special tackle achievement.

On a recent salmon-fishing trip to one of the great Gaspé Peninsula rivers, we found the water low and warm and the fishing poor. A note left me by a friend who had fished there the week before said, "Maybe you can catch fish at the long, deep pool by the road, but no one has taken a fish there for almost a month, and it's loaded with salmon." The conditions were challenging, but I felt I had the answers.

One of the answers was the Prefontaine. I hooked four fish in one afternoon in that long, deep pool on the little #16 Prefontaine and landed two. Another fell to the Prefontaine on a different pool each of the next two days. The only other fish I took in the three and a half days on the river came to the Surface Stonefly. Both the Prefontaine and the Surface Stonefly were flies that hadn't been passed over the fish before, although these salmon had seen a great many other flies in the six weeks most of them had been in the river. The idea of so small a hook as a #16 for salmon keeps most anglers from using them, and the Surface Stonefly pattern was fished by no one but me. The Surface Stonefly is a very effective fly, and I describe it under "Special Flies." When salmon become jaded about the patterns that pass over them day after day, a different look will often stir them into striking.

It was on this trip that Lucien Rolland took his third salmon over twenty pounds on a #16 Prefontaine. He said he did it to show the guides that using it successfully wasn't just a special prerogative of mine. The guides said that if they hadn't seen it with their own eyes they wouldn't have believed that a twenty-pound salmon could be caught on a #16 fly. After we left, two of the anglers that live in the area and fish the river often decided they would catch salmon on the Prefontaines I left with them. The last I heard they had hooked five salmon on them before the season closed and lost them all. But I'm sure these anglers will soon be able to take fish with these wonderful little #16s under the very difficult, low-water conditions when these flies work best.

The Prefontaine works on trout, of course, and it will skate over the roughest possible waters. I grease both line and leader when I fish it, twitching the fly in an irregular fashion. I don't worry about the current, fishing it both upstream and down-

The Fat-Bodied Spider.

Left, Light Coty Stillwater; *right,* Dark Coty Stillwater.

stream. Often I twitch it several times then give it long periods of dead drift over the water I think the fish lie in.

One last Spider variation that I'd like to include here is the Fat-Bodied Spider. Recognizing that the sparse Spiders I tie have the minimum number of hackle fibers (and so the least visibility of hackle fibers) needed to float a hook on the water, it occurred to me that I was missing a bet in not using this almost-invisible flotation to carry a fat body, such as a little, round beetle body, along on the surface. Accordingly, I tied Spider-style hackle forward on the hook shank, tying off the tail as in the standard Spider pattern, and then I added a fat, black or yellow wool body between the hackle and the tail to imitate the body of a beetle. The hackle fibers are few and not very visible, and the fly tends to float flat on the water. The long, spread-out hackle fibers give maximum flotation, and the fish focus on the fat little body floating along in the surface film, just like beetles do. This fly has worked both when there were beetles on the water and not.

A fly similar to the Fat-Bodied Spider is the Coty Stillwater. I tied this fly for the first time shortly after creating the Wulff flies. This fly is different from the Fat-Bodied Spider in that it has short, thick hackles instead of long, sparse hackles. This fly is named after Vic Coty, one of the early dry-fly fishermen on the branches of New York's Ausable. I tied these flies up, one in a dark version and one in a light version, both with blue-dun coloration, while working with Vic after a frustrating experience with some very difficult trout on the Ausable. It's a buggy fly, sort of a plainclothes Adams, and a good fly to have on hand.

SEVEN

Streamers

The first time I used streamers was in 1923. I'd seen a fly called the Rooster's Regret in the Abercrombie & Fitch catalog that came out in January of that year. It had long, white hackles trailing out over a long-shanked hook behind a pair of wound hackles, and it was recommended for bass in the Belgrade Lakes in Maine. It was the first fly of that type that I had seen. I tied up some flies like the Rooster's Regret, and when fishing that year on the Russian River in Alaska I caught more rainbows with that fly than the top guides could catch on salmon eggs.

Streamers were slow to be accepted by the trout-fishing fraternity. Trout were caught on *flies*, and, to many of the old diehards, a streamer was not a fly. In the late 1920s I rarely found anyone fishing a streamer in the Catskills or on New York's Ausable, and overall I think I made more converts to streamers than I did to the Wulff series or to stonefly-nymph imitations.

73

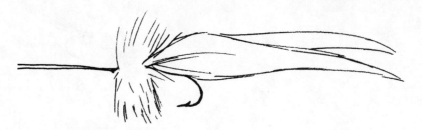

The Rooster's Regret, featured in a 1923 Abercrombie & Fitch catalog.

As late as 1938, when I went to St. John's, Newfoundland, to promote Newfoundland's fishing, no one at the Murray Lake Club of that city—the most prestigious fishing club on the island—had ever seen a streamer. On my first circuit of the small lake at their clubhouse, the rainbows hit my streamer hard, and I made converts out of some of the club members. And whenever I fished for the big sea-run Newfoundland brookies, the local fishermen were amazed at the effectiveness of my streamers, and soon they took off their Black Gnats and Silver Doctors and swore by the streamers I gave them.

Streamers are minnowlike flies, and I love them. Lesser fish are a basic food for almost all gamefish, from trout to sharks. Streamers will fool them all. The streamer represents a good mouthful of food to a hungry fish.

The shape of the streamer is important. It should look like a minnow. A minnow such as the shiner or chub is usually slim and silvery with a lateral stripe. Another common minnow is the darter, which is heavy at the head with wide front fins and tapers in the body back to a small tail. The darter type, such as the sculpin, is adapted to the pockets and bottom waters near rocks and other underwater cover; the shiner or chub type of minnow is typical of the baitfish of more open water. There are many other minnow shapes that fall in between that of the slim minnows and the heavy-headed minnows.

A streamer fly should be light for easy casting, but bulky enough to look like a good mouthful of fish flesh. Like all good flies, the streamer should be as durable as possible. Not all of my streamers are particularly durable; often I sacrifice durability to gain lightness or a particular action. A hair-wing streamer, for instance, with the base of the hairs solidly imbedded in a lacquered head, will outlast a similar pattern with hackle feathers for wings. However, the long hackles are much lighter and easier to cast, and they give a more flexible action in the water. Maribou feathers, too, are not very durable, but they're light and respond to the slightest movement of water.

Many anglers have problems with catching streamer-fly wings in the bend of the hook. If the wings of a streamer are too long for the hook, they can flip around in the current while being fished or in the air while being cast and catch under the hook bend, which will spoil the shape and action of the fly in the water. To solve this problem use either a larger hook for the same sized wing, or a shorter wing. A long wing shape can be achieved by tying in a long tail, which cannot get caught in the hook bend.

Visibility is another important thing in streamers. Although it is good to have a range of shades and colors from light to dark and bright to dull, there is a real advantage to a fly that the angler can see as he fishes. This is particularly true in fast water and pocket water. In these waters the fisherman can give the fly special action

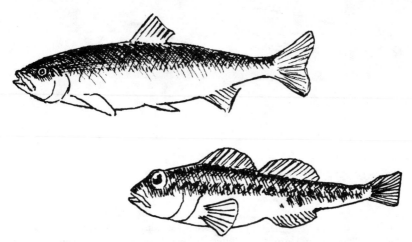

Left, a slim-bodied minnow; *right,* a darter minnow.

Styles of streamer wings.

as it comes to the precise spots where it is most visible to the fish. He can often see the fish strike, or at least he can see the light or bright streamer disappear from view—probably into a fish's mouth. Watching the fly closely can be as important in streamer-fly fishing as in dry-fly fishing. The fisherman who watches his fly will often catch just the smallest flash as a fish

The long-winged streamer shown at top left often results in the wings being caught under the hook bend as shown in top right. Bottom are two solutions to this problem: *left,* using a longer tail and shorter wings; *right,* using a larger hook for the same size streamer wing.

makes a pass at the fly, and he can mark down the spot for another try a few minutes or a few hours later. But if he's just watching the water generally or waiting for a pull on the fly, he'll miss the flash altogether and miss the chance to work longer over a spot that he knows holds an interested fish.

I think the basic charm of a streamer to a fish is the action imparted by the angler. While I've tied up a lot of the standard streamer patterns that originated in Maine, that hotbed of streamer innovations for landlocked salmon, most of the time I take what materials are handy and improvise with them, tying streamers that I think will look good to the fish in a particular area. The classic patterns are beautiful, and I love them, but when I improvise I can fit the flies I tie to the action I plan to give them in the stream. I try to have some part of the streamers I tie made from very soft feather or fur that will move readily in the water.

I have favorite materials, of course. Squirrel tail is one of them. It doesn't enlarge the head of the fly when tied in, and it moves well in the water. Badger hackles are another favorite. They give a streamer that fishy, lateral stripe. I like to make streamers with a bright or contrasting body, something that flashes. I also like a material that will give either a striped or mottled effect to the back of the streamer, which may imitate a chub, dace, shiner or small trout.

Top row: tying streamer with sparse bucktail wing. *Bottom row,* tying streamer with a heavier, squirrel-tail wing.

My streamers most often have a wing base of squirrel-tail or bucktail hair, over which are tied a pair or two of matched hackles. If I use bucktail I prefer the hair of the finest diameter. Using hair as an underwing for the feathers gives the fly thickness and body with little added weight, and it makes the fly usable if one or more of the hackle wings breaks off. I put a bright fin color at the throat, perhaps with the redfin shiner in mind.

A favorite streamer of mine is one that I made up when fishing for steelhead in Alaska. We had been using the typical flies tied to imitate a gob of salmon eggs, which were most successful and should be fished dead drift. Streamers are given life in the water, however, and I felt that a good streamer would be more fun to fish than the natural-drift egg flies.

Using the materials I had at hand in a hastily snatched-up flight bag, which had last been used on a trip to fly-fish for sharks and been supplemented with some trout materials and hooks, I tied a streamer that we named the Kulik Killer, because we were fishing the Kulik River area. The fly has a tail of two long, white saddle hackles, wings of paired, light-yellow hackles, a body of gold mylar chenille and a blaze-orange hackle wound in front of the wings. I used a gold-plated #1 hook, choosing a standard-shank model because I felt those big rainbows would strike hard and take the fly well, not follow and nip the tail. The fly is bright. It is beautiful. And it was sensational the way it took steelhead and char on that trip.

To tie the Kulik Killer, begin by wrapping the hook shank with thread from the bend to near the eye and back to the bend again. Tie in two facing, white saddle hackles for the tail. They should extend a little more than one hook length beyond the bend of the hook. The body is made of gold mylar chenille, which is wrapped from the bend to near the hook eye. Secure it with thread and cut excess. For the wing, two bright, paired, light yellow hackles are tied in over the back to extend to half the length of the tail. This length is long enough to give a good yellow back color, but not so long that the hackles will become caught under the bend of the hook when the fly is cast or fished. To

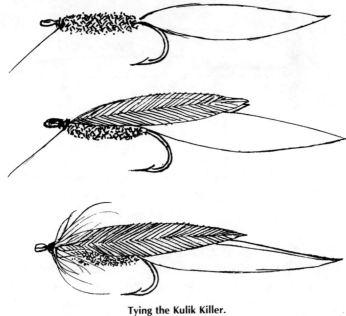

Tying the Kulik Killer.

complete the fly, wrap the head with a soft, flame-orange hackle for six or seven turns.

I have taken brook trout with the Kulik Killer in the Adirondacks, brown trout in Montana, smallmouths and pike in lake shallows and walleyes in the deeper water of lakes, and stripers in the sea. I have faith in it for anything from brook trout to bluefish, and it is one of the flies that I carry on all of my trips. I have not yet caught an Atlantic salmon on the Kulik Killer, but one made a fierce rise.

I like my streamers to be beautiful, and I think of them often as flashing, swimming, almost living things. On occasion in a bush camp I have turned out very prosaic streamers—often just a yellow body with red and white hackles over the back and a yellow tail. On one trip with artist John Groth to the Sutton River, which empties into Hudson Bay, I tied a streamer using red, white and yellow hackles, adding a mixed red and white ring of hackle

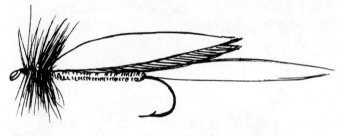

The Picasso.

at the head of the fly to give it a little action like a jellyfish at the head. We needed to bring brook trout up from deep pools of dark water, and that fly did it. John thought it was a work of art and named it the Picasso.

Small streamers are very useful. Often, when a fish has made a pass at a big streamer, either out of hunger or resentment at something invading its territory, that same fish will solidly strike a smaller streamer, such as one tied on a #10 hook.

One way to brighten up a streamer is to break up the color of the body into two parts in the manner of salmon flies such as the Jock Scott. This gives both color and flash and also a different character to the body than most streamers have. While I do try to please myself with a streamer body that is beautiful, I am also hoping that the fish will find such a streamer more attractive than one that has a simple, uniform body. I also often use feathers from a golden-pheasant neck to add a little flash and color here and there on streamers.

Streamers designed to imitate darters should be fished deep in the water, near the stream bottom. These small baitfish are not

One way to brighten up a streamer is to break up the color of the body into two parts, as in many salmon flies.

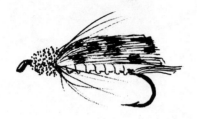

The Muddler Minnow.

like the free-swimming minnows of the open water, and they lack the trim shape of the open-water minnows. The darters are shaped for a quick dart of motion rather than for sustained travel. They have very wide and strong pectoral, or forward, fins and use them for quick propulsion. Their tails are small and their bodies taper quickly from their relatively large heads to their very small tails.

Darters are rarely far from cover, and they are essentially bottom dwellers, choosing the rock crevices and other similar places to hide and dart out from for food. While the other minnows seek safety in shallows, where the trout cannot easily follow them, the darters live in the deeper water, where the trout tend also to live, and they simply hide when not making a quick dash for food. The darter settles to the bottom, pressing against it, and seems to disappear because of its camouflage coloring.

Darter imitations should be fished deeper and slower than most other minnow imitations, and their overall motion is most effective when punctuated by quick jerks or darts on the retrieve. These streamers often work best when tied on a keel-type hook, which puts the bend of the hook up and helps avoid snagging when the fly touches bottom, which it should do occasionally to suggest the darter's hiding and resting periods.

Muddlers can be good darter imitations when fished deep with a jerky motion.

Except for a few special patterns, when I tie up streamers to replace ones that I've lost I tie whatever comes to mind with the materials available. I've made up far too many different combi-

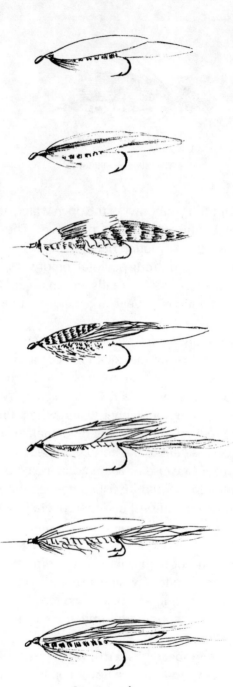

Streamer styles.

nations to have names for them all. I just tie them and use them, and I feel that those I'm using now aren't significantly more or less effective than those I've tied and used in the past. There is one notable exception to this: More and more I am tying streamers on flexible tubes for the advantages the tubes give in lighter weight and a smoother silhouette. I will cover this in greater depth in the next chapter, "Special Flies."

Overall, however, when I look for a streamer, I don't look for a particular pattern. I look for the size and coloration of streamer I feel will work best at that particular time. As in my boxes of drys and wets and nymphs, there will be some streamers without names, some that were spur-of-the-moment creations, some that fit no accepted category and some that sit in the boxes to be tried when the spirit moves me to experiment with them.

EIGHT

Special Flies

In this chapter are grouped several fly innovations. I feel that each one of these flies has its own special use, and that the angler will find that they help solve some of the problems involved in imitating natural insects and baitfish successfully. Like most of the other flies that I describe in this book, these special flies are not strict patterns, but rather systems or categories of flies, and the fly tier should be able to develop his own patterns within these categories to meet his specific fishing needs.

FLEXIBLE FLIES

Among my most recent innovations are the flexible flies, which I wrote about in the January 1978 issue of *Sports Afield*. These flies are the result of bringing together some new solutions to four basic problems of current fly-fishing.

First, I realized that anglers are quite skillful at playing and landing fish and that they could play and land fish successfully on hook sizes much smaller than those they are forced to use by the size of the fly being fished. Anglers are more skillful today than ever before at playing fish; most trout fishermen, for example, have no worry over landing a two-pound trout on a #18 or a #20 hook. I know from my own experience that twenty-pound-plus Atlantic salmon can be landed on a single #16 hook, and I have also landed a 148-pound striped marlin on a 4/0 hook. I realized that if hook sizes were proportionate to the size of the fish, not the size of the fly, fishermen could take most of the fish they hooked using much smaller hooks. The problem was how to tie a fly of a certain size on a hook that was too small to carry the materials for that fly.

Second, I wanted to tie a fly that avoided the telltale down-hanging bend of the hook that signals a fake to fish. This is always a problem with conventionally tied flies.

Third, the long-shanked hook used for many streamer and nymph patterns holds fish poorly. As the pull in the fish's mouth, first in one direction and then in another, is exerted while playing a fish, the long-shanked hook has a leverage that wears a hole where it penetrated. While I had already made some jointed-body nymphs and streamers, which were better than standard long-shanked hooks, I wanted something better.

Fourth, when a fish bites down on a fly and finds the metal core of the hook hard and unyielding, it instantly spits the fly out. That means that the strike must be immediate, or the fish will eject the fly and go free. If the fly could be made to feel as soft as an insect or a baitfish, the fish would hang onto it and the chances of hooking the fish would be greatly increased. For example, the hard-rubber worms of the old days—perfect in shape but too hard and readily ejected by the fish—have been replaced by the soft-plastic worms of today. The soft worms have revolutionized bass fishing; the bass grab the soft worms and hang on. Could I make a fly that trout and other fishes would hang onto until the hook was set?

European tube fly with treble hook.

The plastic tube offered solutions to these four problems. The tube fly of the European salmon angler was developed as a way to use a small treble hook, instead of a much larger single hook to hold a salmon. Treble hooks are illegal on most North American salmon waters, and the tube fly has been almost completely overlooked by anglers here. The European tube fly is made by tying feathers and/or other materials on a plastic tube that is slipped over the leader to slide down and ride against the small, bare, treble hook. The tippet, with the treble hook attached, is then tied to the leader. This is also similar to the way early saltwater "feathers" were made—a lead head with a hole in it and with long hackle feathers attached was slipped over a wire leader to slide back and ride against a large single hook. I felt that I could bring the tube-fly idea to trout streams in an entirely new way.

The flexible fly I developed is tied onto a section of plastic tubing of a type that will accept adhesives. As with the European tube flies, I attached the hook to the tippet section of a leader and passed it through the tube, but unlike the European tube flies, I used single hooks. All throughout one season I tried these tube flies, setting the hooks in the tail or the head, and I kept the flies a secret from all but a couple of close friends. When I knew the flies really worked, I wrote the article for *Sports Afield*.

Any standard fly pattern can be tied as a flexible fly, simply by attaching the materials to an appropriate length of tubing and locking the materials firmly with adhesive. The plastic in some tubing is hard and impervious to most glues and solvents; the tubing I have found satisfactory for these flies may be obtained from Kearsarge, Inc., 13854 Park Center Rd., Herndon, VA

Tying a flexible nymph, weighted with soft lead wire.

22070. The Wilhold (Pliobond) adhesive is excellent for these flies, because it sets up quickly and retains flexibility after hardening. Using this adhesive, wings and legs may be held at right angles to the tubing. Although it can be messy, the results are worth the care. I hold the tube in my fingers when I tie, but for a particularly tricky pattern, insert a stiff wire, such as piano wire or a sewing needle, into a vise and slip the tubing over it.

The greatest advantage of the flexible fly comes with nymph patterns. The fish will hang onto them, instead of spitting them out the instant they feel them in their mouth. The flexible nymphs can be fished free-drift without the angler having to watch an almost invisible leader to recognize the slight twitch that says a trout has taken the nymph. The fish will actually hang onto the flexible nymph until the angler can feel the tension and set the hook. Only when the pressure in setting the hook comes along does the trout know it has taken a fake. This use of tubing for nymphs should have the effect on nymph fishing that the plastic worm had on bass fishing.

There are distinct benefits for streamer flies, too. The smaller hook that this style of tying allows can be set closer to the tail—in the best hooking position—without affecting the length or shape of the streamer pattern. The smaller hook also means that the

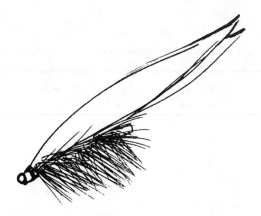

Section of a streamer tube fly, which may be used alone or with other sections to add length.

feathers or fur along the back of the pattern is less likely to get caught under the bend of the hook than in standard-hook streamers.

The silhouette that can be obtained by tying the flexible flies as nymphs or streamers is more realistic than the shape of patterns tied on standard hooks. The flexible streamer is shaped more like a minnow, with no heavy hook bend to break up the minnow silhouette. And the nymph patterns tied as flexible flies don't have the telltale hook bend showing them up as frauds. A few fibers at the right place for a minnow's rear fins or a nymph's legs will hide the small hooks without changing the general shape. On standard patterns, the hook is just too big to hide.

Spent-wing drys also enjoy an advantage with tubes. The combination of the tube and a short-shanked hook is lighter than a standard hook, thus allowing better flotation to these hard-to-float flies. All of the unweighted flexible flies cast more easily than conventional flies of the same size because they are lighter—and the larger the fly, the greater this advantage with tubing.

Using the tube idea, flies can be made up in sections. Additional sections can be added to flies to make them longer, and since the hook is already big enough to land the fish the angler is after, adding size to the fly doesn't mean that a larger hook is necessary. Adding fly sections is quite valuable in saltwater fishing, where large, long flies are often needed. Striped bass, in particular, are very selective about the size of the flies they take, and the ability to change the length to suit the bass can be a real advantage—and the fly can be lengthened with a minimum of added weight. This is much easier than carrying a variety of different-length flies. There is flexibility between the

Flexible spent-wing flies.

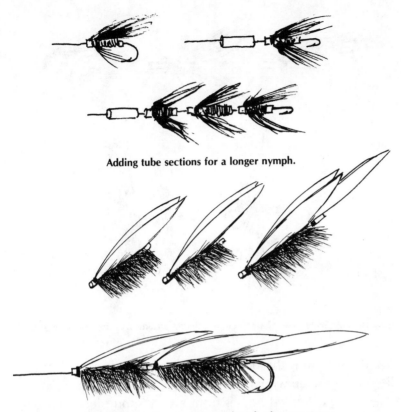

Adding tube sections for a longer nymph.

Adding tube sections to increase length of a streamer.

sections as well as in the individual sections themselves. The
illustrations show how the various sections of a saltwater fly can
be used, as well as how the sections of nymphs and even skaters
can be used.

The tubing can also be used as an extended body, with the
hook set into the front of the tube, either through a slot in the tube
or by permanently tying the hook into that position on the outside
of the tube. While using a fairly large stonefly imitation with the
hook at the head, I was amazed at how few strikes I missed, even
though some of the trout were quite small. The small fish seemed
to strike directly at the head while the larger ones apparently
engulfed the whole fly.

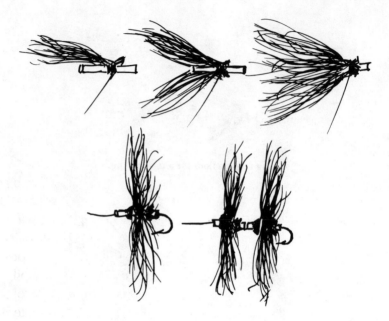

Tying a flexible Skater. Two Skater sections produce an almost unsinkable double Skater.

While writing this book and fooling around with the flexible flies I've come up with another application of the plastic tube in flies—tying extended bodies from a very short piece of tubing, just enough to support the hook properly.

I find I can make a great grasshopper imitation by combining a short length of tube with an extended, looped, polypropylene

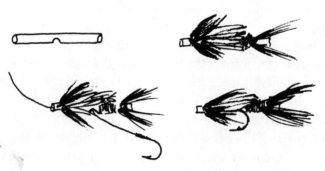

A flexible nymph with slit for hook in middle of tube.

Using the tube for an extended body.

yarn body. The hook bend can be made to ride up or down, but I prefer it to ride up, into the wings, to disguise the hook. To tie the Flexible Hopper, simply secure a length of yarn to the end of the tube, double it back as shown in the illustrations, and secure it. A touch of Wilhold (Pliobond) adhesive to the inside of the polypropylene loop will help the body retain its shape and flexibility. You can finish the fly with looped-hackle legs and hackle collar, similar to the Looped-Hackle Hopper pattern described later in this chapter. This Flexible Hopper, on a snelled, short-shank hook, is light and very easy to cast—and it's soft in the trout's mouth. Any hook size can be used, but I prefer a #10 short-shank hook.

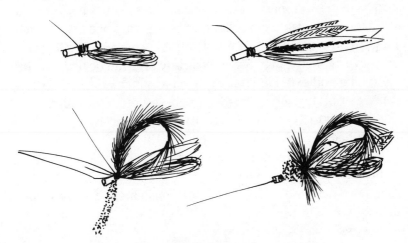

Tying a looped-hackle flexible grasshopper imitation.

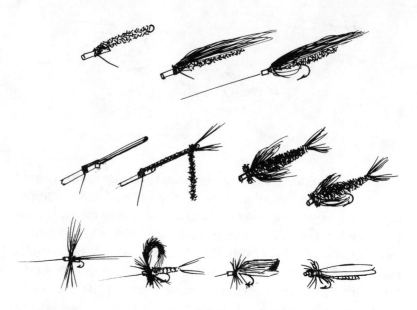

Attach materials to a short tube to form an extended flexible body.

This type of extended body is excellent for nymphs of any sort, especially stonefly nymphs. For short-tube nymphs, a piece of soft lead wire may be extended from the tube and a suitable body can be wrapped on the wire for a weighted nymph. The short tube can also be excellent for spent-wing patterns, using a longer than usual bucktail tail with dubbing or yarn fixed to it with adhesive. Stonefly, mayfly and caddisfly drys can be tied with the short tube and extended body as well as streamers. Even a damselfly can be tied using this technique by securing a brilliantly colored floss to a very long bucktail tail with adhesive and making looped-hackle wings to aid flotation. This damselfly imitation will be relatively fragile, but it will also be valuable when a big trout has refused all other offerings, and only a few casts are required to take the fish. The flexible tube lightens the fly as much as possible, and the snelled, short-shanked hook results in the least possible weight to keep afloat.

Another application for the short tube that I've discovered is

A short-tube, spent-wing fly.

the use of hackles that spread out horizontally and will ride flush on the surface. I call this fly the Crazylegs. To tie it, take four small hackles and place them at the front and rear, one on either side of the tube as shown. The body is then applied between the legs. A variation of the Crazylegs has the hackles at the rear of the tube and the soft, fluffy fibers of a hackle stem at the front. They are tied in and set with adhesive. A second variation bonds two full hackle feathers with the adhesive to the top and bottom of the tube. The fibers of the hackle are pulled out straight and the adhesive will set them in this position. This fly is primarily for use

A short-tube, extended-body damselfly.

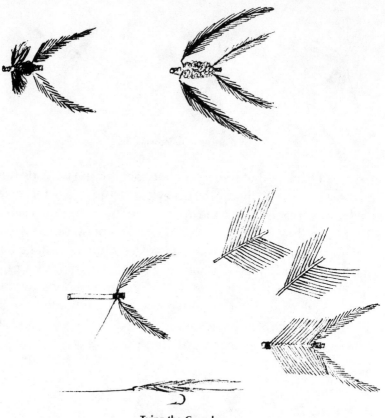

Tying the Crazylegs.

on slow-flowing waters. Fast currents will swamp the fly, and its hackles won't work as enticingly as they should. These flies are so buggy looking and different that they may offer a fish a now-or-never chance to see just how this buggy delicacy tastes.

At first I used the available hooks and had a difficult time getting some that were suitable. It was important to have the hook fit properly into the tube, because it would help the fly keel, or ride upright with the hook bend hanging down. Hooks with turned-down eyes tilted the hook bend up too far, and hooks with turned-up eyes pointed the hook out of the line of pull. A straight-eyed hook would have solved these problems, but the eyes of these hooks were usually too large to slip into the tube.

I could have solved the problem with these hooks by either using a larger diameter tube or slitting the tube horizontally; however, using a short-shanked hook would allow less of the hook shank to slip into the tube, keeping the fly softer overall. I finally found some small straight-eyed hooks, Mustad 3366. They worked well, although they were a little bit longer of shank than I wanted. I finally solved the hook problem completely by cutting off the shanks of the hooks to the length I wanted and snelling them directly to the tippets. I merely roughened the short shanks and set the tippet windings with epoxy to snell them. I have yet to have one of these snells come apart. This gave me hooks that set themselves perfectly in the tail of the tubing.

If desired, the hook may be set anywhere along the tube. A cut in the tube on the side of the fly that is to ride down allows this, and that short section of the tube is kept free of feathers and other materials so the head of the tippet can be inserted easily. Then the hook is pulled into position.

In most cases I make my snelled tippets about two to three feet long. As they are tied to the leader and cut off each time a fly is changed, they gradually shorten. When they become too short to fool the fish, I simply knot on a longer tippet section, and the knot will pass through the tube when the fly is attached.

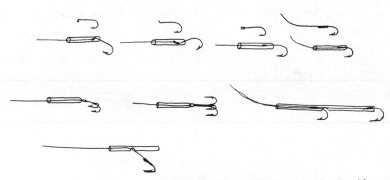

Top row from left to right: up-eyed and down-eyed hooks make the hook point ride out of the line of pull; ring-eyed hook maintains the line of pull but requires a wider tube; short-shanked, snelled hook is the answer. *Middle row:* double hook with tube; treble hook with tube; tube slit to accommodate two hooks. *Bottom:* Tube slit to accommodate hook in the middle.

A flexible streamer with tandem hooks and double tippet.

Double hooks give better hooking in some cases, and a double of a smaller size will hold as well as a larger single. But I dislike doubles because they're more difficult than singles to remove from a fish's mouth, and the handling is more likely to cause injury to the fish. In special cases a tandem hook can be made for a long fly by using a second snell and placing the second hook somewhere in the body of the fly. This would result in a double tippet, with the rear of the fly on a single strand of tippet and the forward part on a double.

In order to weight nymphs and streamers using the full-length tube, the first and probably best method is to simply wrap lead wire around the tube itself, in the manner that many standard-hook flies are weighted. The lead wire is soft, bends easily and returns with the fly to its normal shape without distortion. And, more importantly, it does not take away the softness or flexibility of the fly.

The other method is to slip a soft metal sleeve over the plastic tubing. Sleeves such as these are normally used for splicing wire

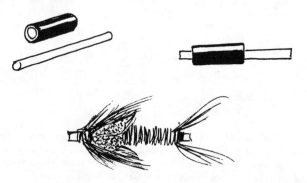

Weighting a flexible nymph with a soft-metal sleeve.

leaders together by passing the two sections of wire leader through the tube and crimping the tube tightly with a special tool. These sleeves may be obtained in various diameters at tackle stores or under the Sevenstrand trademark (Fenwick/Woodstream, 14799 Chestnut Street, Westminster, California 92683). I sometimes tie flies directly onto these metal tubes when a small but very heavy nymph is needed. These metal sleeves may also be slipped onto the leader ahead of a flexible fly to act as a sinker or split-shot.

BACKWARD DRY FLIES

I have a friend who is a "white hunter" in Africa. His clients bag a lot of game because he makes them crawl on their hands and knees during the stalk, even though it seems undignified and is awkward and sometimes painful. If, as with most hunters, they walked upright, the game would recognize them as humans at a greater distance, and the quarry would scram before the hunters could get into good shooting range. Just as a wary game animal can recognize the distinctive head-and-shoulders silhouette that says "man" and "danger," so does a smart trout recognize the telltale bend of a hook that hangs down from most flies. A smart trout is usually one that has been caught and released or has narrowly escaped an angler a few times.

Anglers are so used to seeing the hook bend hanging down from conventional flies that I sometimes think the fishermen expect the fish to look for this, too, as a part of a natural insect. Any fish but a careless one will spot it.

There is a good way to camouflage the hook bend on a dry fly. Unlike wet flies, it is not important what direction the dry fly faces as it comes off the leader, because the dry is not being worked in a specific direction. If a dry fly is tied backward on the hook shank, with the tail coming out over the hook eye and the hackles wound around the shank near the hook bend, the hackle fibers will camouflage the ever-present hook bend.

A backward dry fly.

The backward dry flies can be very effective on old, smart trout. I use these flies in very small sizes on finicky fish, and they work better than the conventionally tied flies. Reversing the fly is a worthwhile innovation that is certain to be used more frequently as trout become harder and harder to fool due to increasing fishing pressure.

Another advantage to the backward-tied dry beyond camouflaging the hook bend is that it is a more efficient way to float a hook. The hackle, the fly's main source of flotation, is placed at the heaviest portion of the hook—the bend. This is a better match of weight to flotation than placing the hackles near the eye of the fly.

Any dry-fly pattern can be tied according to this method by simply reversing the order of the materials on the hook shank.

Another method of camouflaging the hook bend is the keel-type hook. I used to bend the hook shanks on many of my wet flies so that the weight concentration forced the bend of the hook to ride up instead of down. Keel-fly hooks are now commercially available, and flies can be tied with materials that hide the hook bend. Not only does this allow the wet-fly and streamer patterns to have a silhouette that is not broken up by a protruding hook bend, it also helps eliminate bottom snagging when patterns are fished deep.

I also discovered that repositioning of the materials on the hook shank could cause a standard hook to ride with its bend up. I tied a plastic-bodied streamer, which I dubbed Doug's Darter, with bucktail or calftail wings tied to cover the hook bend and pheasant breast feathers spread out at the thorax. The water resistance when the fly was pulled through the water pushed up the hook bend. A fly of this type can be very effective. Once I took some very wary trout, which my companions couldn't interest, by casting this streamer into a pool, letting it settle, and giving it a few quick darts after it had rested on the stream bottom for about a half a minute. I describe how to make plastic-bodied flies later in this chapter.

Doug's Darter, the keel-type flies and the backward dry flies are all effective flies for hard-to-fool trout because they succeed in camouflaging the hook bend that, despite what some anglers must think, signals a fake to smart trout.

LOOPED-HACKLE FLIES

Following up the idea of the backward drys, it occurred to me that I could camouflage the hook bend of a grasshopper imitation with a material that would bend back in imitation of the grasshopper's long hind legs. I was about to go to the West again to fish in the country where a grasshopper imitation is one of the deadliest flies throughout the long period from late summer

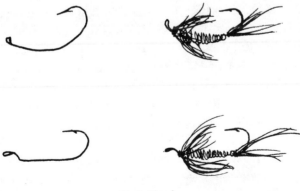

Keeled hooks.

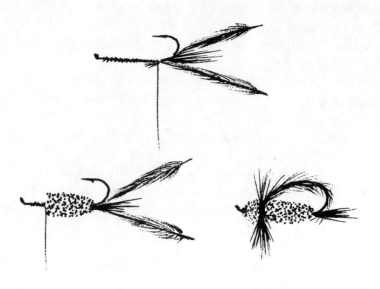

Tying the Looped-Hackle Hopper.

through fall. I was looking for a material for the legs that would be soft, long, springy and would suggest the general appearance of the grasshopper's hind legs.

A loop of hackle gave the greatest promise, and when I started tying experimental patterns I found with pleasure that the looped hackle was springy and had a scraggly appearance, much like the natural's legs. It would also add flotation to the clipped-deerhair body that I planned to use.

To tie the Looped-Hackle Hopper, begin by tying in a short bit of bucktail for the tail and the tip ends of two badger hackles at the hook bend of a 4XL, #8 hook. Secure the tail and hackles with a drop of Wilhold (Pliobond). With the tail and hackle tips secured, spin a deerhair body up the shank to the point at which the thorax will be made. Clip the deerhair to shape. Loop the butts of the badger hackles back to the thorax and secure them with tying thread. Clip excess. Tie in another badger hackle and wind it for a few turns to simulate the forelegs of the grasshopper. Finish the fly with a clipped-deerhair thorax and head.

On some patterns I laid a short wing down the back between the two looped hackles, but I decided the looped-hackle legs made the wing unnecessary because the fish couldn't see the wing. I also tied some patterns with a few turns of hackle in front of the head, near the hook eye, but I decided that this, too, was unnecessary. The facing hackle was not needed for flotation, which was accomplished by the looped-hackle legs, clipped-deerhair body and hackle fibers at the thorax.

This looped-Hackle Hopper worked well for me, and I'm certain that it took some fish that would have been put off by the conspicuous hook bend hanging down from a conventional pattern. The Looped-Hackle Hopper floated well, resting in the surface film, and its legs had a lifelike movement when twitched.

The looped-hackle idea might have stopped here, with the grasshopper imitation, if I hadn't been doodling on a pad at the International Salmon Advisory Group meeting in Montreal six months later. Suddenly, while thinking of salmon and their various survival problems, the thought flashed through my mind that perhaps the loops of hackle with their strength and springiness had other, better applications. I sketched out a moth with looped-hackle wings, and felt that I had devised, for the first time, a good, durable imitation of the many moths that float along with outspread wings in a delta-shaped configuration.

As soon as I got home I started to work on mothlike flies with looped-hackle wings. I came up with a spruce moth type of fly and imagined it floating over a big salmon or trout. I was certain from the look of the thing and the way it floated in a bowl of water that any fish would hate to miss a chance of rising to it.

I made up some moth patterns with two pairs of wings instead of a single pair of wings for better flotation. I wanted the fly to lie flat in the surface film. I made the first bodies out of clipped deerhair, but I found that the wings would float a body of wool or chenille just as well. I tied some with hackle wound around the head of the fly, at the hook eye, and decided that a few turns of hackle there simulated insect legs very well. I like these flies best with grizzly, badger or furnace hackles for the wings, because these materials may give a mottled effect and a striped effect.

When I gave motion to the fly in the bowl of water the wings had a fine, springy action. They tightened toward the body on the forward move and sprang back into position as soon as the fly came to rest. The action was so good that I decided to try looped hackles on still other types of flies.

I made some big bass bugs that I knew would be good, and I made up some dragonflies that would float on slender looped-hackle wings and a short spread of bucktail for the tail. Other patterns came to mind, and I tied them as I thought of them. Eventually I used looped hackles on wet flies, streamers and even nymphs. Tied as a short loop in the front of a streamer, the hackles

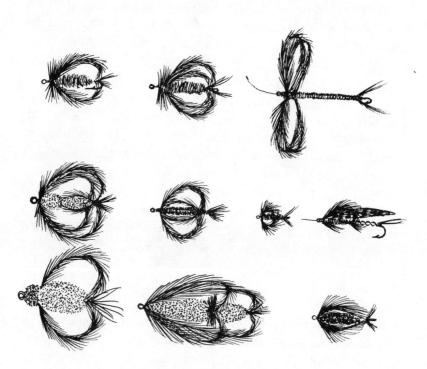

Looped hackle moths, nymphs, streamers and bass bugs.

gave a Muddler effect to the head; tied as small forward loops on a heavy, sinking body the hackles made an imitation of a darter. In each of the different patterns illustrated, I counted on the resilience and liveliness of the loop hackle to make a fly that floated or looked better than conventional patterns. It was quite an exciting tying session!

When I finally floated that original Looped-Hackle Spruce Moth over a big salmon, he rose to the fly beautifully, and I felt that old, warm glow that comes when a fly of your own creation excites a good fish into taking. The possibilities of looped hackles for flies are far-reaching, and over the years I expect looped hackles to find a place among the standard patterns for trout, salmon and bass.

THE WRETCHED MESS

At one time Joan and I were directors and instructors for the Garcia-American Sportsman's Club fishing school on the Elk River at Steamboat Springs, Colorado. Breakfast at 7 A.M. was followed by a full day of fishing instruction. In the evening, after dinner, I taught a tying session until about 10:30 P.M. Many of the students had fished only a little or not at all before attending the school. The fly-tying sessions were well attended, with the instructors tying and most of the students staying up to watch.

A student asked, "What materials and tools do I need to start fly-tying?"

My response was, "A vise, hackle pliers, scissors and thread. Get a few hooks from some fly-tying friends, and for materials, get those friends to give you the stuff that they throw away. If you want to start by tying flies for trout, you should start with tying nymphs, and the materials that most tiers throw out will be fine for practice and even for very good flies. Here," I continued, "I'll show you."

I scanned the pile of tying scraps that was going to be thrown out after the evening session. I picked up a 2XL, #8 hook. "This," I said, "you'll have to buy, or bum from a friend. Now, for thread,

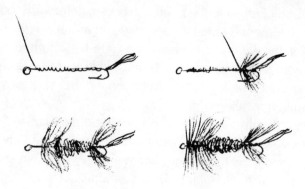

Tying the Wretched Mess.

your wife's fine silk will do for the larger flies, but for the small sizes you'll need special, fine thread. Right now, let's stay with the big flies."

Scanning the pile again, I found some scraps of soft, yellow feather, and I tied them in for a short tail. Then I picked up the butt ends of some badger hackles that had been used earlier for the hackles on a Wulff. The furry, fuzzy stuff at the base of such hackles is soft and alluring, and it is almost always thrown away. I call it "poor-man's maribou," for it is as soft and flowing as the expensive maribou feathers. Pulling off two tufts, I tied one on each side of the hook at the tail, spread out like the hind legs of a lizard or an insect. Next, I picked up some ends of dark gray and black yarn, and, mixing them, wrapped a body on the shank. At the head I tied on another pair of "poor-man's maribou" legs, spreading them out on either side of the shank like the hind legs. To finish the fly, I tied in a few turns of a furnace hackle that had no tip and had thus been discarded. I tied the fly off and said, "There's a scrap fly that will catch fish."

"What will you call it?" one of the students asked.

While I was trying to think of a name, my friend, hard-fishing Charlie Meyers of the *Denver Post,* sat shaking his head and muttering, "That's a wretched mess!" And so it was named.

The next day I took as many trout on that nymph as I did on any other fly. Today, it, or a variation of it, is always in my fishing

vest. It looks like a bug, and it seems alive in the water. It is true
that few underwater things, except salamanders and frogs (which
the Wretched Mess certainly does not imitate), have pairs of legs
at the front and back. Insects have six legs, and crawfish have ten.
But just as the artist enjoys an artistic license that allows him to
depart from reality to achieve a sense of motion or some other
special effect, so the fly tier need not stick to reality in his
imitations. The artist uses his license to please himself, his view-
ers or his clients, and the fly tier uses his license to entice trout. I
have included the Wretched Mess in this chapter because it
represents a fly that proves this important point, and also because
it shows that successful flies don't have to be tied from the
materials the catalogs list as the best materials. The fly tier should
never lose sight of either of these aspects of fly-tying.

FORM-A-LURE PLASTIC-BODIED FLIES

In the late 1940s I got the idea that making flies could be
simpler and less time consuming than conventional tying proc-
esses allowed, and in 1950 I patented the idea of imbedding fly
materials in a plastic body that could be secured to a hook shank.
I made molds in cold, hard steel in which I could make poly-
styrene bodies that could be secured to a roughened or humped
hook. I could embed fly materials in the body using a special
plastic solvent so that fibers would project from the body at any
angle I desired.

I figured that tying flies by hand with thread was the equiva-

The Wretched Mess.

lent of drilling holes and riveting sheets of steel together as the construction workers used to do before the process of welding made the rivets obsolete. I saw that imbedding materials in a plastic body would permit making flies to become, to a large extent, an assembly-line procedure, and I started a business.

I made ants on #12 and #14 hooks, streamer flies on #2 through #10 hooks, and wet flies on #4 through #14 hooks. The flies in the wet categories were great, and I caught a lot of fish on them. But I made drys, too, and they were not like conventional drys. I floated them on flat hackles or on hackle wound parachute style around a plastic stub protruding from the body.

It was a business that showed promise, and I felt it should have grown. I had partners, and we all tried. But not hard enough. I was too busy with writing, running a salmon-fishing camp and giving lectures to devote the time to our business that it would have taken to get the idea off the ground. Only the plastic-bodied Surface Stonefly has showed any degree of permanence as an established fly pattern.

In terms of selling the flies, I made a serious mistake in not following conventional patterns in the streamers with this new idea. I remember showing a display card of the plastic-bodied

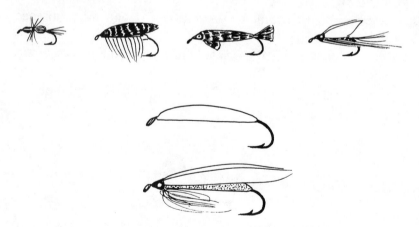

In the middle, the plastic body; patterns of plastic-bodied flies.

streamers to a fisherman who came up to the booth at a sportsman's show. He stared at the flies intently, and then he shook his head. "They won't work," he said, talking to no one in particular.

"They do work," I said. "What makes you think they shouldn't work?"

"The fish won't take them, he replied flatly. "You haven't even got a Royal Coachman streamer there."

"Do you think the fish would take a fly with a body like this if it were tied as a standard Royal Coachman?"

"Yes," was the reply.

"The fish can't tell whether the body is wool or plastic by looking at it. I could make Royal Coachman streamers as easily as any of these patterns. But I'll tell you something: These patterns look more like minnows, and if a fish recognizes a fly as a Royal Coachman and not a minnow, he won't take it no matter what the body is made of." I couldn't convince him.

Then there was a flood, and all the molds were lost. The business went to hell. I bought a new plastic machine and made a few molds to continue producing the very effective Surface Stonefly, which had become one of my secret weapons for Atlantic salmon and a specialty for big trout when the conditions were right. I made plastic-bodied flies for my own use, and my stepsons even turned out some as a way of making money. There is still a demand for the plastic-bodied Surface Stoneflies. Over sixty percent of the salmon taken on one of the north-shore rivers in Nova Scotia one season were caught with those flies. Although the anglers in the club on that river had imitations made without the plastic bodies, they didn't seem to work as well. The demand for the Surface Stoneflies continues.

To make the Surface Stonefly I cut matched bucktail fibers of the proper length, dip them in a combination of plastic and solvent, place them just behind the vertical stub of the plastic body, and let them set. Once the solvent has softened the plastic enough to accept the fibers into it, I press the butt ends of the bucktail firmly into the plastic and shape them so that the fibers

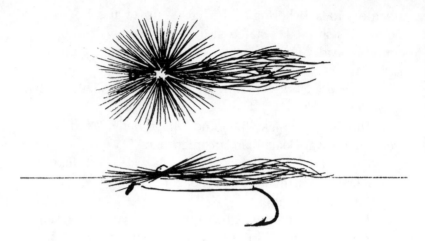

The Surface Stonefly.

will form a flat fan over the back, in imitation of a stonefly's flat wings. Then, holding a hackle stem in position around the vertical stub, I put solvent on the stub and wind the hackle around it. The fly is hung on a pin with a pair of hackle pliers holding the hackle in place until the solvent has set. When the solvent has hardened, the hackle tip is trimmed and the fly is finished. No thread! No tying!

The parachute hackle at the head gives it a lifelike motion when pulled through the water, the body is slim, and the bucktail is typical of a streamer fly. But it is as a dry fly that I use it most.

The Surface Stonefly is the salmon fly I would hate most to give up. I developed the fly specifically for salmon. I felt a real need for such a fly, because my old standbys, the Wulffs, had become so popular that they gave me no special advantage. The salmon were seeing enough Wulffs already, and I wanted a fly that was a departure from Wulffs and the other conventional Atlantic-salmon flies.

I have been partial to stonefly imitations ever since I used live stoneflies for trout in the late 1920s. I knew that stoneflies existed in the salmon rivers as far north as Ungava Bay, so in the search for something that would interest salmon, but was not yet available on the market, I thought of imitating a hatched-out stonefly.

Wet flies are most successful in early-season, high-water conditions. I wanted to create a dry fly to meet the challenge of taking salmon in late-season, low-water conditions. My first attempts were with a long, wool body and a conventional hackle at the head. They worked, but it was hard to get them to float flat in the surface film. If well greased, they rode too high on the water; otherwise, the wool body became soaked and hung the tail of the fly so far down in the water that it looked unnatural.

My next attempt was with a plastic body with a conventional hackle at the head, but the hackle tended to hold the head too high. By changing to a parachute-style hackle imbedded in a plastic stub on the body, I could get the whole body down into the surface film while it floated on the hackle and wings. This is the pattern I settled on.

Still, this fly is hard to float, and most of the people I first gave it to fished the fly wet—and they swore by it as a wet fly, if they gave it a good trial. In order to fish the fly as a dry fly, it has to be skidded to the surface. I land the fly like I land my seaplane: I slide it onto the surface. If I simply cast it out and let it drop six inches or a foot in a free fall as with most drys, it would break the surface tension and sink. It is an expert's fly, actually. It can be floated by a side cast, a cast to within a few inches of the surface or sometimes by smacking it down hard on the surface and letting it make a small bounce that gives it a gentle, final drop. When it does float, it floats so low in the surface film that it practically sinks and it is very difficult to see. But somewhere in the minds of salmon there must be a memory that it triggers. The Surface Stonefly has caught a great many fish for me—fish that I couldn't catch with other flies.

Normally, with a mixture of grilse and salmon in a pool, it is easier to get the grilse to rise than it is to bring up the salmon. The Surface Stonefly, however, tends to get more rises from the larger fish. This fly turned out to be great for me when I was running a salmon camp, because I wasn't able to fish until late in the day and only in places where other fishermen had fished hard before me. If I were going to catch salmon, I had to come along and catch them behind some very good fishermen who had the expert knowledge of my guides to help them. The Surface Stonefly helped me to do this.

Tied in smaller sizes, on #8 or #10 long-shanked hooks, the Surface Stonefly is very effective for trout. These may seem too large by conventional standards, but even some of the very smart trout in the Beaverkill's no-kill stretch have been fooled by them. In the West, where grasshoppers and large stoneflies are part of the standard diet of trout, they are also effective.

Another of the plastic-bodied, no-tying flies came in handy in Iceland. I'd made up a fly that had a shrimpy look, with orange hackle feathers laid horizontally along a yellow plastic body with the hackle fibers projecting downward. Two mallard feathers faced out from each side of the back.

With a new guide and a new river in prospect, I put the fly on and showed it to my guide, Hjamar. He shook his head and said, "It won't catch salmon here." I persisted in fishing with it, and

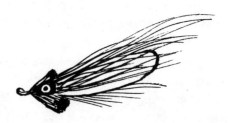

Top, Stuart's Swimmer; *bottom,* Doug's Darter.

within five minutes I hooked and landed a salmon. Then I took the fly off, opened one of my boxes of conventional wet flies, and asked Hjamar to choose a fly. I wanted his complete cooperation, but I also wanted to fish my own experimental flies on occasion. I figured that by proving right off that my experimental flies would work, my guide would be piqued to prove that his time-tested favorites of the river were better. It worked, and I had marvelous fishing with him.

Overall, however, there are only three plastic-bodied flies that I still use consistently. They are the Surface Stonefly, Doug's Darter (which is described earlier in this chapter) and Stuart's Swimmer. Stuart's Swimmer has a squirrel-tail wing, which gives a medium or dark, white-tipped effect to the wing, and a spread hackle feather imbedded in the bottom of the plastic body to give a soft, fringy action along the bottom of the fly. This fringe action of the hackle is one of the advantages of the imbedding process; it allows action within the fly when it is moved at minimum speed and gives one of the better imitations of an insect's legs.

Most fly tiers will probably not go to the trouble of making up form-a-lure plastic-bodied flies. But the fly tier that does will be able to take advantage of some of the unique effects made possible by this technique.

NINE

Flies for Bass and Lake Fishes

Flies for the lake fishes are minnow imitations for the most part. The streamer is the universal fly for such fish as bass, pike, muskies, walleyes and lake trout, and bright colors are generally in order. For bass, however, flies of all sorts—including those that imitate such things as frogs and newts—are also effective. For panfish, small, fat-bodied bugs are usually best.

The Kulik Killer, which I describe under "Streamers," is as good for pike and bass as it is for Alaskan rainbows and Labrador brookies. It is bright, flashy and fishy, and I use it more than any other fly when lake fishing. Another favorite of mine is a streamer tied as a flexible fly, because it allows me to lengthen whatever pattern I'm using by adding sections to it. I use the flexible streamer for big fish, and I describe how to tie it and how to add the sections under "Special Flies." When fishing for pike and muskies, which have sharp teeth, I use the flexible streamer on a

Spinner and streamer combination for lake fishes.

wire tippet and can add sections easily by slipping them over the wire. Whatever the streamer pattern chosen, adding strips of silver mylar tinsel to it will make it more attractive to most lake fishes, because the tinsel will make the pattern resemble a minnow more closely. A small spinner ahead of the fly may also be added to give flash, although the spinner adds weight.

Many of the saltwater flies are good for bass, pike and muskies. I often use the typical Florida tarpon fly with hackles wound ahead of two pairs of spread and trailing hackle feathers. This fly has a tantalizing action when brought in just under the surface with an erratic retrieve.

With bass there's quite a bit of variation. Smallmouths will take small flies better than largemouths. One of the nicest surprises I can remember was a strike that came to a #12 Black Gnat while I was fishing the run into Sysladobsis Lake in Maine. In this

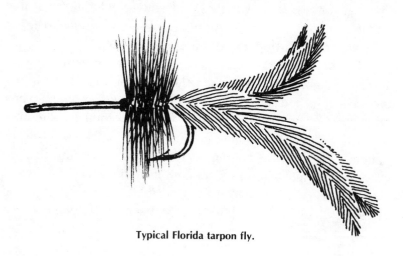

Typical Florida tarpon fly.

lake there was a variety of fishes that might rise to such a fly, including chub, yellow perch, white perch, brook trout and landlocked salmon. But the strike came from a three-pound smallmouth bass, and, until he jumped, I was sure I had a land-locked salmon.

I use #2 and #4 White Wulffs and Gray Wulffs for both largemouths and smallmouths. While both respond, the smallmouths respond better, especially river smallmouths. I have often made Wulffs as large as #1 or 1/0 with fat, clipped-hair bodies for largemouths. In deep cover or in cloudy water, the sound of a bug that size landing on the water—the splash and commotion—will attract bass from a greater distance than a fly just as large but not as heavy. With bass you always seem torn between choosing a light fly for ease of casting and a heavier one for the commotion.

When bass flies were first made, they were simply big trout flies of the old, conventional, European type. The Rooster's Re-

Early bass flies and bugs. *From top to bottom:* the Wilder-Dilg, the Call-Mac, the Devil Bug, the early traditional bass fly.

gret in the 1923 Abercrombie & Fitch catalog was the first streamer I saw, and it was designed for smallmouths. Among the first bugs on the market was the Wilder-Dilg bass bug, which had a bullet-shaped cork head with hackle feathers trailing behind. The Call J. McCarthy Call-Mac bug was also among the first bugs. Its bullet-shaped cork was reversed, with the greatest diameter at the front. Bucktail wings were tied in at the head of the Call-Mac bugs to lie along each side, and feathers were used to brighten up the top of the bug—mainly, I think, to look attractive to the angler, because the fish couldn't see these feathers from underneath.

An early hair bug was designed by E. C. Tuttle, from the Adirondack area of New York, and it was called the Devil Bug. At the sides this bug had bucktail folded back with some of the hairs protruding, at the front, some clipped hair. This created a mouselike face. These bugs were lighter than cork, and they floated almost as well. To this day I use some of the old Tuttle Devil Bugs with as much faith as for any other bug for bass. I have just recently learned that the Eppingers, who make the popular Daredevil lure, have revived and are selling the old Tuttle Devil Bug.

A great fly for bass, especially smallmouths, is a Skater. It is possible to skate a light, bushy, high-floating fly, such as a Wulff, but the best fly for skating is one made up for the purpose. I make my Skaters with enough body so they seem to the bass like something worth catching, and with enough good, strong, wiry bucktail fibers spread around the shank to let it skip along even when there is a fairly good ripple on the water. A bass makes almost as much commotion as an Atlantic salmon does when it takes a Skater, and anyone who bass-bugs has a pleasant surprise in store if they've never tried a Skater. I wouldn't want to go bass fishing without some Skaters in my fly boxes.

Colors don't seem to matter in Skaters for bass. While I've found brown bucktail as effective as any other color, red, white or yellow makes the flies easier for the fisherman to see and, just possibly, a bit more exciting to the bass.

I have a special bass fly I call the Skidder. It's a combination

Top, the Skidder; *bottom,* a skidding streamer.

of a bug and a big Skater. I tie a bug with a Skaterlike head to make the Skidder, and I fish it on a greased line and leader.

To make the Skidder, first select fine, strong bucktail-tip fibers and tie them in for a tail. Next, wind on and clip to shape a deerhair body. This body can vary from a long, slim body tied on a long-shanked hook to a short, round body tied on a standard shank hook. Using the strong, wiry bucktail fibers again, make a fan of fibers around the shank just behind the hook eye. The plane of this fan of fibers should be tilted so that it comes forward ahead of the hook point. This helps the fly ride with the hook point up when worked across the surface. A wall of thread built up in front of the fibers, well set with lacquer, helps the fly maintain its shape even when it has been fished hard.

A streamer-type fly, or something with a body less bulky than the clipped-deerhair body, could be tied behind the Skaterlike fiber fan. It would have a slimmer silhouette and a slightly different action when fished. Long hackle wings trailing out behind a Skater head can be very interesting for bass and pike.

The big Skater head keeps the fly high on the water, and the trailing hair or hackle feathers gives the fly substance. It goes over the weeds and pads like a charm, and, while it doesn't have much splash, it throws a good shadow and must look to a bass as if it contained a fair amount of nourishment as well as being something fun to catch. It flips out easily and has a lighter, faster action than any other fly or bug in my box. The upward-facing hook keeps the fly weedless in spite of the wild yanks I give it.

Walleyes can be readily taken on bass bugs and surface streamers during the hours of darkness, although they tend to seek deeper waters during daylight. Casting with sinking lines and fishing the slow retrieves it takes to stay deep with a fly is never as much fun to me as fishing with surface flies, and most of my walleye fishing, therefore, is done at night. When there are both bass and walleyes in a lake, night fishing can be great sport. The wind is usually down during the night, and fly-casting conditions are often perfect.

Fly-fishing on lakes is always a bit uncertain. How pleasant it is or how successful you are depends to a great degree on how hard the wind blows. I used to take both a plug-casting outfit and a fly-casting outfit with me when I fished Saratoga Lake in New York. If the wind wasn't blowing a gale, I'd fly-fish, and if it was, I'd take up the casting rod. Not only does a wind make fly-casting difficult, it also makes the fly or bug on or near the surface hard for the fish to see.

Using a high-density sinking fly line or shooting-taper is a good way to get the fly down quickly when there is no surface activity. A fly-and-spinner combination, using a spinner that will

A streamer tail fly with a streamer dropper looks like a school of minnows.

revolve with a slow retrieve, is a very effective way to fish big streamers deep.

My first muskie taken on a fly was in Algonquin Park in 1933. It was a twelve-pounder. I remember the fly: It was a white hackle streamer with a silver body and facing head feathers of golden-pheasant tippets. I had a single small spinner ahead of it, and the fish was, at the time, one of the largest fish I'd taken on a fly rod. Since then there have been many other large muskies and pike, and I think that fishing for either of these fish is great sport.

One of the special tricks I have tried and have found useful for lake fishing is putting a dropper streamer about six inches ahead of a tail streamer. Lake minnows are found more often in schools than are the minnows of rivers and streams, and two flies look more like a school than a single fly does. I've even followed this thinking further and used three streamers, each about six or eight inches apart. But three flies are a lot more likely to become tangled, and I decided the third wasn't worth it. I have found the two-fly combination a very good one, and it is certainly more visible to a hungry fish and, I figure, twice as tempting. One pike I took on the double-fly rig took both streamers in one gulp, coming up from behind with mouth agape. I think, however, that most fish tend to take one and plan to keep an eye on that second meal while they turn the baitfish, swallow and savor it.

The panfish, such as bluegill, sunfish, rock bass, yellow perch and others have small mouths. Small, fat-bodied bugs, either floating or sinking, are more effective for these lake fishes than long, feathery flies or heavily hackled flies. The panfish often

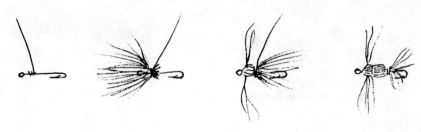

Tying a bucktail bug.

miss large flies on the strike because their mouths are so small. It's almost impossible to take a panfish on a Spider or a Skater. Fishing floating bugs for panfish can be great fun, and, as with the other lakes fishes, I prefer it over fishing for them with sinking flies.

A very effective bug can be made up quite easily with bucktail that will work for panfish and also for very wary trout. Wrap a bunch of bucktail fibers to the hook shank near the eye, tips pointing forward. When the fibers are secured, they can be bent back to the tail and tied in, forming an insectlike body. If a few hairs at the tail and at the head are left free to flare out, they can act as legs for the fly. If you tie the fibers tightly near the hook bend, they will also flare out to suggest legs.

These bugs look like terrestrials of some sort, and they have proven very effective for trout, but they are very good bugs for bluegill and other panfish because they can be tied in small sizes quite easily and have fat, buggy bodies.

Saltwater Flies

Some years ago, when working on a proposed "Mako on a Fly" segment for the "American Sportsman" TV series, my first responsibility was to convince the producer that a shark would take a fly. He felt that if sharks would take flies, people would be fishing for them with flies and fly rods. He believed that sharks took meat. Period.

I explained to him that the main food for any predatory fish in the sea was other fish, that sharks were no exception and that a streamer fly was the best baitfish imitation possible. I told him that sharks would take streamers like a kid takes candy. Still, the producer had to be shown, and so we set up a test trip out of Montauk, New York, at the easternmost tip of Long Island. It was a one-day trip, and while we weren't lucky enough to see a mako, a one-hundred-pound blue shark came into the chum slick, up to the boat, took the fly and was subsequently boated.

We spent four days shortly after that attempting to catch a mako on a fly, but we never had one come into the chum line. We did catch a couple more blue sharks, and while we were playing one in the skiff, with sound cameras rolling and communications cut off from the main camera boat, a broadbill swordfish came into the chum slick and took pieces of fish tossed over to it. Had we known that a broadbill had appeared, we would have cut off that blue shark and raced back to the main boat to get a fly to it. Hungry broadbill within fly-casting range are as rare as miracles, and I would have loved to have been the first angler to catch a broadbill on a fly. I have cast a fly to a broadbill off Panama, and to another one off Ecuador, but both had their minds on other things, paying no attention to the fly or to the baits we put to them later.

Fly-fishing grew out of trout fishing and matching the trout-stream insects, but over the years we have taken flies and the fly rod to all the seas of the world. Flies can be effective on practically all saltwater fish. I've caught flounders and cod on flies. I've had an eel come up and take a streamer, not only in saltwater but also in a salmon pool. Many of the saltwater fish live in deep water, and reaching them with a fly calls for weighted lines and long-delay retrieves, which takes fishing for these fish a long way from the fast-moving, delicate casting the fly fisherman enjoys on a trout stream.

There is a point beyond which it becomes questionable if fly-fishing can be used to take big fish. I feel that big bluefin tuna are so strong that any known fly-fishing tackle would be insufficient to subdue them. The rod required to cast would have to be double-handed and heavy, and playing a thousand-pounder would have to be done from a swivel chair—a far cry from fly-fishing as we know it today, and as it has been practiced over the centuries.

There is a basic difference between freshwater and saltwater flies; there are no marine hatching insects that can provide food for the fishes. Most freshwater flies have been inspired by the freshwater insects, while most saltwater flies have been inspired by baitfish. The common ground between freshwater and saltwater flies is the streamer fly. A few saltwater flies, however, are designed to imitate crustaceans or marine worms.

The first saltwater flies were the "feathers," although I wonder if these patterns should be called flies. The feathers were made up of a bunch of long hackle feathers attached to a lead head, and they were used for trolling. They were weighted to take them down a bit below the surface, and their action was essentially that of a streamer fly.

Saltwater fly-fishing, as we think of it today, was developed by freshwater anglers who took their fly tackle to saltwater. Famous salmon fisherman Howard Bonbright first fished for tarpon with flies much like those he used for Atlantic salmon. Gradually, saltwater fly designs began to develop, starting with streamers and spreading to hackle-wrapped hook shanks with a pair of spread hackles tied in at the tail. Bucktail streamers, somewhat similar to those used for bass and pike, came along to add variety. Popping bugs, such as those used for bass in freshwater, were found to be attractive to some saltwater fishes, and anglers began to use cork-headed poppers, some with long tails, for sailfish, tarpon and snook.

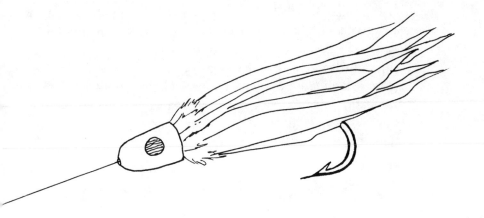

A saltwater "feather."

The Sea Wulff.

In making up flies to fish for a striped-marlin record in 1967, I wanted the longest, softest fly I could contrive that would still be light enough to cast easily. I came up with a tandem fly, using two 4/0 lightweight hooks joined together with sixty-pound-test nylon. This fly had a lot of hackle feathers blended together into a long, slim shape. It was light and had excellent action in the water. I wanted to break away from the long-tailed popping bugs that were popular at the time among the few anglers who fly-fished for Pacific sailfish. The popping bugs had a single hook at the head, and I always felt that a cork body mounted on a hook tends to affect the hook's bite, making it more difficult to set the hook at the strike. While I lost the excitement of the popper's splash and action by tying a fly without the cork, what I gained in extra size for the same weight and in hooking qualities was worth it.

We called this fly the Sea Wulff, and it became a standby for me with other big saltwater gamefish, such as tarpon and sharks. It is a good tarpon fly when the water is cloudy. For sharks I connect the hooks with wire instead of nylon. As with some of my flies for Atlantic salmon, I use the nylon between the hooks as a continuation of the hook shanks and tie feathers to it, integrating the fly's parts and creating a long, complete fly with a very flexible action.

Tandem hook made by attaching hooks with monofilament, using a blood knot.

Using the Sea Wulff I caught a record striped marlin of 148 pounds on the second day out. We made a great movie for the "American Sportsman" series. The twelve-pound-test record still stands as the largest marlin caught on a fly.

Taking the record marlin was part of my effort to show that fly-fishing is mainly a game of skill. There is a generally accepted feeling that such a fish requires a multiplying reel with a heavy drag and a strong, double-handed fly rod. To prove that a skillful angler could take such a record fish with simple tackle, I used a *single-handed* fiberglass fly rod, weighing just under five ounces (and costing, incidentally, less than twelve dollars), a single-action fly reel with a click (only to keep the spool from overrunning), a standard ten-weight floating fly line and 350 yards of nylon backing. Drag was applied with finger pressure, and the rod was held in my right hand with the butt against my right forearm. Woody Sexton was my guide, and we fished from a fifteen-foot skiff with a thirty-five horsepower outboard engine. We were fifteen miles offshore, near Salinas, Ecuador, and the fight lasted four-and-a-half hours.

While I also use the long marlin tandem flies for tarpon, most of the time I use the typical flared feather streamers for this gamefish. Sometimes I tie these flies with thread, and other times I fix the feathers at the bend of the hook in a small, plastic body. Another good tarpon fly is the flexible streamer fly, because of the lightness of this streamer for casting ease, and because it may be lengthened by adding more sections. When fishing for sharks, and other fish with sharp teeth that require a wire tippet, the flexible streamer sections can be slipped over the wire shock tippet.

I use 4/0 light-wire, nickel-plated hooks or typical return-looped-eye Atlantic-salmon hooks, gold-plated sometimes, for most saltwater fish. Bonefish flies are best if tied on #1 and smaller hooks, because this makes the fly easier to cast, and the fly splashes less when it lands near an easily spooked bonefish.

I've made up bonefish flies with plastic bodies, embedding the materials so that the hook point rides up. Ordinary hooks may

A plastic-bodied bonefish fly.

be weighted to do the same. Bonefish are bottom feeders, although they are swift and will take a fly at any depth. In fact, in 1947, when fly-fishing for bonefish was just beginning, I took one of my first fly-rod bonefish on the surface with a bass bug. Still, the best place to put a fly is where the fish is looking for food, and with bonefish that means on the bottom.

Striped bass are one of the better fish of the sea for fly-fishing. They are caught mostly on minnow imitations, and the size of the fly tends to be critical. Stripers come into sheltered waters, which are best for fly-fishing, although the fly fisherman can take them right in the rolling surf in relatively calm weather if he knows where and when to fish. The striper fly should match the baitfish of the area or a small eel. As with most saltwater flies, a flashy material is a help with striper flies, and silver or gold mylar is worth using to brighten up the flies. Mylar is light, tough, durable and flashy.

The amount and type of motion given to a saltwater fly is a matter of choice. The mere fact that the fly moves is important. Erratic movement will draw attention at a greater distance than a steady swim. With bonefish, it makes sense to let the fly sink to the bottom in the shallow water ahead of the fish and give it a twitch of life as the fish approaches. Having once seen it move, the bonefish will sometimes pick it up while it is motionless on the bottom, just as a freshwater bass will often take a motionless bug if it has seen it move.

Saltwater fly-fishing is an exciting frontier that we're still exploring. The flies I've described in this chapter are not merely specific patterns for the specific gamefish mentioned. They are good saltwater flies that may be varied in size and shape to take many of the other fly-rod gamefish of the seas. There is great sport in fly-fishing for bluefish, bonito, mackerel and many other fishes. The angler should remember that, as with freshwater fish, the look of the fly, the inherent motion its materials have and the motion imparted by the angler are keynotes to flies that saltwater fish will take. There are different challenges involved in tying saltwater flies—primarily incorporating bulk and length to a pattern that is light enough to be cast—and the suggestions I have made can be effectively adapted for most saltwater fish that can be caught on flies.

ELEVEN

Choosing Atlantic Salmon Flies

I'm always interested in water and fish, whether I'm fishing or not. Whenever near water, I start wondering if there are fish in it, what kind they are, and what might interest them enough to make them strike. One of my standby methods of determining if there are fish in nearby streams or rivers employs the coin of the realm. Anywhere that I can see down into the water, I'm willing to risk a penny or more to find out if there are fish. I toss a coin out and watch it flutter down through the water; if there are gamefish around they'll usually show up to take a look at it and sometimes to take it into their mouths. Nickels are bigger and brighter than pennies and can be seen from farther away by the fish, and they're worth the investment if you're really interested in knowing if there is a predatory fish nearby. In many cases dimes are best because they are lighter. They sink the most slowly and flutter most.

I started this monetary fish-calling in 1933. Several of us

131

were standing on a bridge over the Ecum Secum, a small Nova Scotia salmon stream, where the water flowed in either direction with the tide, to and from a long, brackish lake that lay at the foot of the river. The resident anglers said that it was foolish to fish for salmon there because the salmon were neither in the sea, where they might take a herring or a big streamer that looked like a herring, or in the fresh water, where they might revert to the taking of insects or insect imitations.

As we were standing on the bridge talking, a ten-pound salmon came in from the sea, bucking the out-going tide. It settled into a slow-current lie within our sight. Our tackle was back in camp a hundred yards away, and I couldn't see anything handy, such as a cigarette butt or a short piece of rotted wood, to throw in to the salmon to see if he would strike. Searching my pockets I came up with a quarter and a dime. I flipped the dime about thirty feet across the stream to land a few feet upstream of the salmon. The dime sank, fluttering and sending silver shafts of light back to us from under the water. The salmon surged forward at the glittering coin, missed it, and made a lightning-quick turn to catch it before it reached the streambed. There was a flash a moment later as the fish ejected it, just as salmon are supposed to do with flies.

That little piece of silver told us that, in spite of local tradition, salmon *might* take a fly in that brackish-water run. So we fished there hard for several days. While the season had been very poor, due to low water and reluctant fish, we took more salmon in that place where they "couldn't be caught" than we did in the usual fishing pools upstream. All because of a lucky dime.

I have no problem choosing between wet flies and dry flies my first day on a new salmon river. I use a wet fly. It will cover more water than a dry in the same period of time, and it will let me move more and see more of the stream to study its character.

If conditions are normal, I may choose a typical salmon fly, such as a Jock Scott, Blue Charm, Silver Gray, Thunder and Lightning or a Black Dose. But it is more likely to be a less widely used fly, such as a Haggis or a Lady Joan—flies that are not likely to have been passed over the fish by other anglers.

The Haggis is a fly that I made up while in Scotland, and I named it after haggis, a Scottish dish made from oatmeal, liver, blood and some other ingredients. I made the fly up while fishing in a contest with British salmon angler, Donald Rudd. The most famous of their angling writers, Rudd had a pen name of Jock Scott. He was using a long, heavy rod, and I was using a short, light one; the contest was big rod against small rod for Atlantic salmon. This took place in 1962, and I won over Rudd, one ten-pound salmon to none. I took that fish on a dry fly.

While I didn't take the contest-winning fish on the Haggis, I did take two salmon on that fly while fishing the Dee. I lean toward dark flies, particularly on dark days, because fish see flies silhouetted against the light of the sky. During that week in Scotland the skies were almost always low and dark. So I made up the Haggis, which I intended to fish on a riffling hitch, which was unknown in Scotland at the time. (I describe how to tie and use the riffling hitch later in this chapter.) I wanted to put something new and different over the relatively stale fish of late June. The Haggis is a black fly, with a flash of silver tinsel and a touch of bright yellow at the throat. I also added a few long, wiry, black hairs from the tip of a bucktail to give extra flotation without increasing the bulk of the fly's materials. I knew I could skim that fly through the roughest water at the pool heads using the riffling hitch, where a normal salmon pattern would swamp if skimmed.

Since I created the Haggis it has been one of my favorite and most effective salmon flies. I tie it both with the long, fine, wiry, black bucktail hairs for extra flotation and without them when the extra flotation isn't needed, such as when fishing the fly in a normal wet-fly fashion. The Long-Haired Haggis is a better fly, too, for skimming over relatively still water, where the current is not strong enough to hold up a normal, riffle-hitched fly.

I created the Lady Joan when fishing one of our great northern salmon rivers. I had come across some burnt-orange silk floss that someone had given me at one time. We were discussing colors one night, and talking about those colors that had been particularly effective. Orange was one of them, and I thought of the Orange Fish Hawk, which is a particularly effective trout fly. I didn't have any salmon flies with orange in them, and so I decided to make up some using the burnt-orange floss.

The body of this fly has oval, gold tinsel ribbing wound over an orange floss body. The tinsel gives the fly extra flash. I add a double hair wing, using soft, black-bear hair for the lower layer with the same amount of squirrel-tail hair for the upper wing layer. This makes a good, dark wing with a dramatic white tip where the squirrel-tail ends. I put bright, soft, light yellow fibers at the throat to give a lively supplement to the orange body. As I do with the Haggis, I use an even mixture of the fluffy fibers found at the base of the hackle stem and normal soft hackle fibers. This gives both durability and maximum movement within the fly itself.

A third fly that I use a great deal for salmon is one that I first called the Silver Birch. I later renamed this fly the Cullman's Choice, after a very good friend. This fly has a bright, apple-green, floss body, which is similar in color to the new green of birch leaves in the spring when the fish first come in. The body is ribbed with golden, and a black-bear hair wing is added with a silver-pheasant crest feather topping it to give shine. The black-bear hair allows a smaller head than would bucktail hair. Next I add a throat of soft, white hackle to finish the fly. At times a green fly, such as the Green Highlander or the Cosseboom, is very effective, and the Cullman's Choice fills this niche for me without being too similar to the other green flies that the salmon usually see. I like to give the salmon something it hasn't seen before.

If a conventionally styled fly, such as the Haggis, Lady Joan or Cullman's Choice doesn't bring a rise, then I switch to some less conventional flies. First, I'll usually try a plastic-bodied Surface Stonefly fished wet to cover the category of Muddler-type flies. I make the Surface Stonefly in several color schemes, all with a yellow, plastic body. I tie the Surface Stonefly with an olive bucktail wing and badger hackle, with a brown wing and furnace hackle, with a white wing and badger hackle, and with a black wing and grizzly hackle. My current favorite color scheme for the Surface Stonefly is the olive bucktail wing with badger hackle, although my favorite can change with each season. Again, I'm always making up different combinations of colors for this fly with the materials handy, just to have a variety available.

These flies are my first choices, and if they don't succeed then I start digging into the hundreds of flies I carry, seeking something that pleases me at the moment and will, I hope, also please the salmon. In high water I like a big fly with a silver body; in low water I like low-water flies, generally dark ones. I carry a fairly wide color variety, and when a fish shows an interest in a particular size I will try varying colors over that fish.

When I switch to a Surface Stonefly fished wet, or a Muddler, I usually go to a larger size than I was using in the standard patterns. For instance, if I take off a #6 low-water Haggis I will go to a #4 Surface Stonefly or Muddler Minnow. I believe that each type of salmon fly has a preferred size under normal conditions, although it is not always the same size.

One of the things leading up to the long-rod/short-rod contest was a question from Donald Rudd as to why I used such large dry flies in low water. He, like practically all the other salmon anglers at the time, used only small flies of any kind in low water. Their reasoning, I believe, was that since only small wet flies worked under low-water conditions, small dry flies were also in order under those conditions. These anglers thought that in midsummer salmon only took small flies. I reasoned another way.

Most underwater insects reach maximum size and tend to hatch out in the spring. When these larger flies have gone, all that is left in the way of nymphs are the eggs or the smaller, new crop of nymphs that will make up the next spring's hatch. If, as I believe, the salmon are "remembering" their feeding habits as parr, they will not expect big nymphs in midsummer. So the smaller wet flies work. On the other hand, the land bugs of the summer are getting bigger and bigger with the hot weather as the season progresses. Large grasshoppers, bumblebees, craneflies and beetles begin to fall to the stream, which seems perfectly natural to the fish. So I go to big dry flies at this time of year, using the Surface Stonefly in #2 and #4 far more than any smaller sizes, and I use Wulff flies up to #4 and even larger on rare occasions. These big flies have given me a lot of fish when other anglers, using the conventionally small, midseason drys, were having little luck.

Another type of wet fly just now coming into vogue for Atlantic-salmon fishing is the nymph. The Woolly Worm is proving to be a pretty good salmon fly. As well as my Surface Stonefly, I have also been using stonefly-nymph imitations for salmon for many years. Now I often use a flexible-fly version of a stonefly nymph to avoid playing a fish on a long-shanked hook.

You should always fish for salmon with fly patterns that you have faith in. There will be hours and days when only faith will keep you fishing. When luck is bad, and faith wanes, you should try to stir your own curiosity as well as the salmon's curiosity. You should think, "This fly intrigues me. Maybe, today, it will intrigue the salmon, too, listless as they seem to be."

Ragged flies are often better than crisp, clean, new ones. This holds particularly true of the complex, traditional patterns. These standard flies are expensive, and as works of art are made with great precision. Show me a slightly ragged Jock Scott, however, that has caught a few fish, and I'll show you a fly that some angler has a great deal of faith in. When a few feather fibers have been bent or have broken down, when the silhouette of the fly in the water is no longer sharp and hard, and when the angler has great faith in it, the fly becomes most effective. I've fished with flies so chewed up that it was impossible to tell what pattern they were originally, and these flies still caught salmon. I think the smart angler will tend to tie or use flies that have a slightly ragged look. I remember seeing a very good salmon fisherman take a new fly out of his box and stamp it into the dirt under his heel a few times before he tied it to his leader.

One famous British angler, A. H. E. Wood, caught salmon on

bare hooks with painted shanks, just as I caught trout on bare hooks on the Ecum Secum. Very slim flies work well for salmon, as do soft, worn flies, and the characteristics of slimness and softness can be very important. Worn flies are both slim and soft, and either of these characteristics could mean the difference between a rise and a spurned fly with a particular salmon.

This success of worn and slim flies may be the reason why simple hair flies, which are replacing old, complex, feather patterns, are being used so successfully today. My effort is to tie flies that have beauty as well as built-in casual effect. Often I use a hair-wing base with a light overlay of feathers to get both qualities.

In recent years fishing the dry fly for Atlantic salmon has been one of the most exciting phases of angling. Dry flies for salmon did not become popular with Americans until Colonel Monell, George LaBranche and Ed Hewitt started fishing them half a century ago, but dry flies had been used for salmon in England before World War I. It is a field that is still developing and in which new ideas are still coming along frequently. There is much more to be learned about fishing the dry fly for Atlantic salmon than there is about wet-fly techniques, a field that has been studied intensely for years.

Hewitt's Bivisible was the first truly popular dry fly for salmon. Few people carry the pattern now, but it is a very good fly and should be in every salmon fisherman's vest. The Wulff series came next, and for years they were almost a secret weapon for those anglers who fished with them, because most Atlantic salmon anglers were so dedicated to the traditional wet fly that they would use nothing else. The Wulff became one of those flies that could excite a salmon after the salmon had become jaded toward the traditional patterns.

The Wulffs are still my basic dry-fly patterns for salmon because of their combination of effectiveness, durability and good floating characteristics; all other things being equal, they are my first choice in dry-fly time. While I use the White Wulff, Gray Wulff and Royal Wulff for salmon, overall I believe I use the

White Wulff for more hours than the others, with the Gray Wulff second and the Royal Wulff third. I tend to fish the White Wulff and the Royal Wulff as searching patterns, and I fish the Gray Wulff as a follow-up fly when the fish rise to the other Wulffs but fail to take them. My usual choice is a #6 or #8, but I've used the White Wulff effectively in sizes as large as 3/0. I used such a large White Wulff just to show how large a dry fly salmon would take, but usually I fish this fly in #4 or #6.

My second dry-fly choice for salmon is the Surface Stonefly. Because so few anglers use this pattern, I am certain that when I use it no one else has shown the salmon such a large, slim fly that floats in the surface film. I tend to use the Surface Stonefly when I have had a fish rise to a Wulff that wasn't hooked, or after a Wulff has failed to get a rise.

My third dry-fly choice, which becomes first choice when waters are very low and the fish jaded and reluctant, is the Skater. It is likely to be a Prefontaine if the conditions for playing fish are reasonable for a #16 hook. If the waters are difficult, or for a less experienced angler, I recommend a bucktail Skater on a #12 or #14 hook. The standard Skater does not have the special rolling action of the Prefontaine, but the bucktail I use on the Skater will support a heavier hook in rough water. The action a Skater should be given on the water surface is something that you must learn for

Top row from left to right: Surface Stonefly, 3/0 White Wulff. *Bottom row:* Coty Stillwater, Skater, Midnight.

yourself. I twitch the fly in the way that would be most appealing to me if I were a salmon, and usually I'm thinking of salmon lying in particular spots under the Skater as I work it across a pool. I want the salmon to think that the Skater is something alive, but more than that I want them to be teased into a chase.

A small, black fly called a Midnight, on a #12 hook, made up of two black hackles, a fat, black wool body and a tail of black hackle fibers, is a fly I often use in the chain of patterns I vary over an interested fish. I am most likely to put it on right after I've been fishing a large Wulff, giving it a try between the Wulff and the Surface Stonefly.

I change flies according to the mood I'm in when I'm fishing over a fish that has risen. I think of flies as the keys of a piano: One person sits down and punches keys at random and makes a discord, another chooses keys that make a melody. I think the changes of patterns and the number and lengths of drift of each over a fish can be like a melody to a salmon that finally draws his acute attention and then a rise. Throughout the changes, I revert periodically to the fly that brought the first rise. I know the salmon had an interest in that particular fly, so I keep returning to it, like a theme in a melody, and always as a final offering—as the last fly before I give up. If a salmon rises to a second fly during my offerings, then I have two themes to which I can return, and in which I know the salmon is interested. I work around these themes, trying something in between in size and color before I break away to something contrasting. I have had as many as twenty rises involving eight different flies, before getting the fish to take the fly solidly and feel the hook.

Another effective fly is the Bomber. This fly is simply a long-shanked hook with a clipped-hair body and a hackle wound palmer-style over the body. Years ago it would have seemed ridiculous, and salmon anglers would have been ashamed to have such a pattern in their boxes. It is extremely popular at the moment, but like the Bivisible, its heyday may soon pass. But my recommendation, as in the case of the Bivisible, is to keep a Bomber handy in your fly box always.

Where most other anglers may use the Bomber, I often use a Looped-Hackle Spruce Moth. It, too, has a clipped-hair body, and it will stay afloat, although soggily, through almost any water. Because of the nature of this fly's wings, light will shine through them as it does with most insects. This is a very buggy fly.

Another clipped-hair body fly for Atlantic salmon is the Rat-Faced McDougall. It was one of the earliest clipped-hair flies for trout. It came out of the Catskills and became one of the first special terrestrial-insect imitations to be successful. I had a friend, Gerry Curtis, who lived on the Wye River in Wales, and he used the Rat-Faced McDougall as his only dry fly for salmon. He was one of the few successful dry-fly fishermen for salmon in Great Britain at the time. This fly has the bulk of a beetle but its wings, which are grizzly hackle-point tips, do not resemble a beetle's wings. But it certainly has looked like a bug to a great many fish! The Bomber may well have been inspired by a Rat-Faced McDougall fished by an erstwhile trout fisherman on the Miramichi. Most of the conventional dry flies used for trout will take salmon. I've caught Atlantic salmon on trout flies such as Quill Gordons, Cowdungs, Coachmen and Orange Fish Hawks. I caught one salmon on a clipped-hair fly-rod mouse while trying to take a big trout, and I even caught a salmon on a cigarette butt impaled on a hook, which was a little reminiscent of today's Bomber.

Another piano key that I like to use in constructing a melody to play over the salmon is the Portland Creek riffling hitch, or "riveling" hitch as the Portland Creekers called it. I did not invent the riffling hitch, but I did bring it to the attention of the angling world in an article I wrote for *Outdoor Life* in 1946. The hitch developed in an unusual way at Portland Creek in Newfoundland, where I went to set up fishing camps right after World War II.

The British Navy, which for a long time ruled the seas of the world, included among its officers many who were or wanted to be Atlantic-salmon fishermen. It was a top sport among the British gentry, and aboard every British naval vessel of consequence there were salmon fishermen, and there was salmon-fishing tackle. Whenever a vessel stopped near a salmon river, officers who wanted to fish came ashore. This happened occasionally at Portland Creek during the 1920s and 1930s.

These officers were often poorly paid, and were consequently not very generous with their tips to local salmon-fishing guides. They sought out locals to show them the pools on the salmon rivers, and when they left their tip, it most likely was a fly or two. This was fine when the fly was a modern one with a return-loop, steel eye, but it was not so fine when the gift fly was an old one with a tired, gut eye-loop. It seemed to the Portland Creekers that no matter how many steel-eyed flies an officer had, he always seemed to find a gut-eyed relic when it came to leaving a tip. When the local anglers tied into a salmon with their strong leaders and heavy, spruce-pole rods, the gut eye was almost certain to pull out and leave the fisherman with neither salmon nor fly. In most communities the local anglers either saved the gut-eyed flies for souvenirs, or they threw them away. The Portland Creekers, out of ingenuity or ignorance, came up with a way not to lose their flies or their fish. They tied on the gut-eyed flies as they would any other fly, and then they tied them on again with a pair of half hitches behind the head of the fly, which gave a good grip directly to the shank of the hook.

Portland Creek had an excellent run of salmon, but these fish had always been particularly difficult to catch. When the anglers hitched their flies, the flies skittered across the surface instead of swimming along beneath, and the hook canted off at an odd angle. The salmon came to this skimmed fly with greater abandon than they had ever shown when fished for with conventional tactics. Realizing that they had something, the Portland Creekers began taking half hitches behind the eyes of their steel-eyed flies, too.

My first day at Portland Creek was an interesting one. I had just come from the Humber River, where, a day or two earlier, I had had trouble in getting my wet fly to sink on the retrieve across the glassy surface of the Quarry Pool. It had seemed to me at the time that no salmon would take a fly that dragged across the surface and wouldn't sink. I finally made it sink by holding the rod very low and sometimes even putting the rod tip underwater when I made the retrieve. Watching a Portland Creeker skim his fly across the surface *on purpose* and seeing a salmon take it was a bewildering experience for me.

My local fishing companion hooked several fish while I went without a rise. While I was fishing conventionally, a strong wind came up, and on one of my casts my locking leader loops skimmed across the surface while my wet fly, twelve feet behind it, stayed underwater. A salmon smashed up at the leader knot, giving the line a tug before he let go. I took it as a sign from above, hitched my fly the way my companion's was hitched, cast again and caught the salmon.

I believe that in Portland Creek at the time ninety-five percent of the fish taken on wet flies were taken using the Portland Creek riffling hitch. I brought the first dry flies to the river, and we found that they could be just as effective, but the normally fished wet fly, which worked everywhere else, was a poor fishing method there.

We took the hitch to the other rivers on which I had camps in that big, northwest Newfoundland area, and we found that although the hitched flies worked as well as conventional wet flies, they did not work any better than the usual wet flies. Since then I've tried the hitch on many rivers from Scotland, Norway and Iceland to New Brunswick, and I have always had it work on the salmon. The riffling hitch works on trout, too. I've used it for trout in both the East and the West. It works particularly well on steelhead, helping to take fish that have refused a normally fished wet fly or streamer.

The fish that come to a hitched fly usually come with a surge. The strike is as exciting as the strike to a dry fly. A fish often pokes his head all the way out of the water in taking a riffling fly, and this is a truly thrilling sight. Some of my salmon-fishing friends are now like the Portland Creekers were when I first arrived there.

These friends fish the hitch almost exclusively, and they hate to change and fish a sinking fly because they cannot see a fish take it.

If I raise a fish on a conventional fly, and he won't come back, a change to the riffling hitch will usually bring him to the steel. Sometimes it works the other way, and a fish that shows an interest in the hitched fly, but will not take it, will succumb to a wet fly fished under the water in a conventional manner. The mechanics of the hitch are simple. Tie the fly on with your normal knot, and then make two half hitches behind the head of the fly. The farther back on the hook shank the hitch is made, the higher out of the water the fly will ride; the closer the hitch is to the hook eye the lower the fly will sink in the water. If the water you are casting over is flowing to your right as you face it, the hitch should come off the fly's right side. If the current is flowing away to your left, it should come off the fly's left side. A single-hooked fly will lie flat on the water as it hitches, and you want the hook point to be downstream, facing toward the fish and the direction the rise will come from.

With a double-hooked fly, the hitch should come off directly below the eye so that the fly will ride with both hooks down. Double-hooked flies, standard flies and low-water flies all have

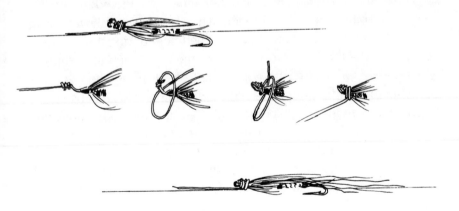

To tie the Portland Creek riffling hitch, simply take two half hitches behind the hook eye. The tippet should come off the side of the fly.

different shapes. Each presents a different silhouette to the fish, and often a fish that refuses two of the types will succumb to the third, whether the flies are riffle hitched or not.

Outside of varying the size and shape of the fly to be hitched, I have one further suggestion. Try tying in a few long, dark bucktail hairs, the fine and wiry type from the tip of the tail, over a normal pattern so that those hairs extend another complete hook-shank length behind the fly. This extra area for the fly to ride on when hitched and skimmed across the surface will let the fly work through rougher water than a standard fly can. The addition of these bucktail hairs does not change the fly's silhouette significantly.

In order to skim properly, the fly must travel at a certain speed through the water. If pulled across the water too fast it will skip and throw spray and not be as attractive to the fish. If pulled too slowly, it will become soggy, and it will sink or lie too low in the water. Fortunately, the best speed for skimming seems to be about the same speed that salmon like to take a conventionally fished fly, too.

In any given year, certain flies and certain methods will take most of the salmon. And during those years some salmon will be taken by bizarre and unconventional flies and methods. Perhaps a good ratio would be to fish about ninety percent of the time with flies that you have faith in, and experiment during the other ten percent of the time. Do your experimenting when the fishing is poorest. Of course, the ten percent of the time when you are experimenting, during the poorest fishing period, means you're actually giving the experimental flies and methods about one percent of the chance you are giving to your favorites. But do not forgo experimenting, because most anglers do not experiment enough. All too often when a salmon fisherman says he's "tried everything" he's only tried the few flies he has faith in.

Thoughts on Flies and Fly-Fishing

In 1930 I moved to Louisville, Kentucky, to be art director at a branch of a large advertising agency. I thought of the job as temporary because agency people were always moving around from company to company as they made their way up the ladder. It was a good job, and I was being paid a hundred dollars a week, a very fine salary for a young man at that time.

When the month of August came along, after I'd been at my new job for six months, the weather was hot and sticky. There were a lot of mosquitoes. Out of desperation I dug up a small can of Lollacapop, a paste repellant made from tar oil, citronella, pennyroyal and a few other things. It was a standby insect repellant for the fishermen in the bush, and I'd always used it to keep bugs away while on the northern trout streams. When I located the Lollacapop and smeared it on that evening, its familiar odor

145

reminded me of the trout streams of New York, and that evening my thoughts stole away to those beautiful streams.

Fishing in Kentucky hadn't been too exciting. There were a few small, shallow ponds that held bass. The Ohio River, which flowed past my door, held bass, too, and it was fun to fish, but its grayish waters were not comparable to the clean trout streams of the Catskills and Adirondacks. While Kentucky's Lake Herrington was in existence at the time, the rest of the impoundments that make today's fishing interesting in that area had not been created.

When I went into the office the following day Bruce Farson, office manager of the agency, gave me the news that everyone would have to take a ten-percent pay cut beginning the first of September, just two weeks away. In my mind I smelled the Lollacapop again, and I saw rising trout on the West Branch of the Ausable. I said to Bruce, "To hell with the cut, and to hell with the job. I can still get in ten days of fishing on the Ausable before the season closes!"

So I returned to the Ausable and reconfirmed that the Gray Wulff would work when the late-hatching gray drakes were coming out and that my streamers would still take big fish. Then I went to New York City, tired but refreshed. I bought a new suit and started to look for a job.

The bottom had fallen out of the job market, and the Depression was a reality. The first areas to suffer were those in the arts and advertising, which always take second place to production and other phases of business. I ended up taking a job with the Du Pont Cellophane Company in the new Empire State Building for a salary of thirty-five dollars a week. The cellophane division was doubling its sales every six months, and it was cutting its employees' salaries ten percent every six months, too. But I still counted myself lucky because of what some of my friends in New York had to put up with to hold a job, if they had a job to hold. This took my heart out of becoming a business tycoon. I figured it would take someone more hard-hearted than I to be successful in the business world. I made my decision then, but it was still six years before I could break away from New York, move to the banks of the Battenkill on the Vermont-New York border and manage to support myself and my family by combining freelance art work, fly-tying and writing, filming and lecturing about fishing. I remember catching a four-pound native trout in the Battenkill's Sheep Pasture Pool the year I moved up there. The few of us in the area who were dedicated fly fishermen had that wonderful river to ourselves for many years. It was better to be happy and poor.

Fishing has certainly affected my life, especially fly-fishing for trout. Its challenges and rewards, problems and solutions, have always captured my imagination and stimulated my creativity.

A while back I served on a committee for the Federation of Fly Fishermen. We were appointed to try to work out a definition of fly-fishing. Our chairman decided that the task was impossible and gave up. But I felt, and still feel, that it is ridiculous for an organization with that name to find itself unable to define the sport that brings its members together.

To define fly-fishing, let us first say that a fly is a lure made of feathers, yarns and other materials that does not have any device built into it or used with it to give the fly action. Its only action must be to follow the pull from the angler or the action given to it by the current. A fly has no stiff lips or other devices to make it swerve, dart, spin or wobble.

Next, we can break fly-fishing down into several classifications, depending upon technique. The first classification is surface fly-fishing, with floating lines and no weight of any kind, in the fly or on the line. The second classification is intermediate fly-fishing, in which weighted flies or sinking-tip lines are used, but no attached weight, such as split-shot or sinkers. The third classification is unlimited fly-fishing, in which lead-core sinking lines, weights and sinkers, and weighted flies (and perhaps spinners) are used.

Of the three classifications of fly-fishing, surface fly-fishing is the most difficult way of taking trout and all the classifications of fly-fishing are more difficult than spinning. With surface fly-fishing, *all* the fish have to be brought to the surface for the lure, and *all* the deep flowing water is sanctuary for the fish. Any trout caught by surface fly-fishing leaves the sanctuary of its own volition, and unless it leaves, it cannot be caught. This eliminates the drifting of a lure right into the trout's holding level and almost right into its mouth, so that simple curiosity as much as hunger may cause it to mouth the lure. The intermediate fly-fishing classification gives the angler a greater advantage and allows him to drift his flies deeper in the flow, where most of the feeding by the trout is done. The unlimited fly-fishing classification lets an angler have maximum advantage, allowing him to reach the fish at their holding level, and this is particularly deadly on big fish.

When I was growing up in Alaska, where there were no game laws, of all the trout-fishing methods I liked spearing best. In conventional fishing methods, you don't even have to see the fish you catch in order to catch it. You can throw out a fly, bait or lure and have the fish find it, take it and be hooked. But to spear a trout you must know where it lies and see it, or, as we often did, drive the trout upstream or downstream until it comes into the shallows and then tries to dart back around you. Then we had the exciting and difficult task of striking a fish with the spear as it sped by at speeds of up to twenty miles an hour. We had to allow for the refraction of the water, which made the fish seem deeper than they actually were. Also the current could move the spear off its

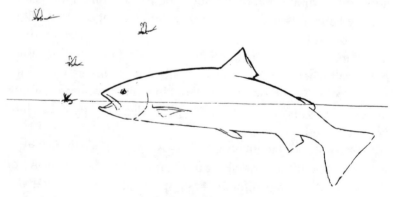

Surface fly-fishing.

Intermediate fly-fishing.

point of aim and affect the proper lead distance ahead of the moving fish.

A beginner might throw his spear a hundred times and never touch a trout. But once he developed the skills and timing needed, he could become deadly—so deadly that a few good spearers could clean all the good trout out of a stream in a very short period of time. Eventually spearing was outlawed, as it should have been. And by the same token, any method of taking fish that is too deadly should be barred.

What is too deadly? That depends on the number of fishermen a particular water or waters have to accommodate. In Alaska in my youth, with only a few of us and a seemingly endless supply of fish, spearing was considered all right. But with spearing or any other method of taking fish, when a lot of fishermen are on a stream, we have to cut down the number of fish each fisherman is allowed to take.

One of the big problems of keeping enough trout in our streams was introduced with the advent of spinning. Spin-fishing allowed anglers to put a lure or bait in the parts of a stream that had previously been sanctuaries for the trout. These were areas that the fly fisherman could not reach. The heavy spinning lure could quickly sink down to the level at which the trout normally lie, and this made it easy for the fish to take a lure for which they

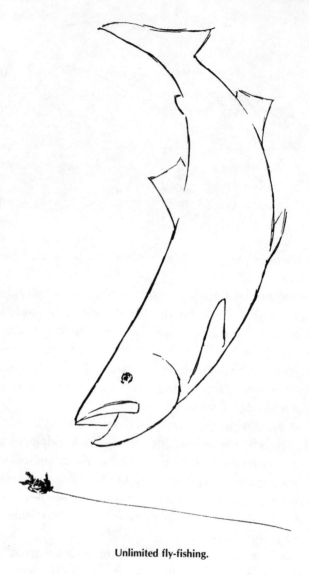

Unlimited fly-fishing.

wouldn't have to come to the surface. Spinning also let anglers cast worms and live baits that would have snapped off on a long cast by a fly rod. Spinning is too deadly for most of our best trout streams, but fortunately a realization of this is giving us streams where spinning, like spearing, is outlawed—thus keeping more fish in the streams for a longer period of time.

Naturally an angler can release his fish regardless of the fishing method he chooses. There will be fish mortality due to improper handling by the fisherman in some cases, but catch-and-release fishing is the best method of maintaining trout populations in our waters. However, a fish that enjoys a sanctuary and is not caught because the angler was unable to fool it, doesn't have to face the chance of injury in release, and it certainly can't be killed by the fisherman.

In my opinion, one cannot compare the delicate beauty of casting a feather-light fly on an unweighted line and leader, softly dropping it to the water, to the casting of a heavily weighted fly or a section of lead-core line. Fly-fishing is a sporting method of fishing in itself. Some types of fly-fishing give the fish more chance and the angler less, and therefore I feel those more difficult methods are most challenging and sporting.

Tying the flies for our sport is like any other complex endeavor. The tier should learn the rules before he breaks them. He should be able to tie the time-tested conventional patterns neatly and well before he starts to bring studied carelessness into his work. Flies have character and fly tiers give it to them. As a fly tier develops his feeling for the look of a fly, it begins to show in his work. The flies of an individual tier may be as distinctive as the work of a painter. Jack Atherton claimed he could spot one of my Wulff flies without fail among a great many other Wulffs tied by other tiers. He could do that with the flies of other tiers he used regularly, too. What makes a fly distinctive may be the way it's finished off at the head, the balance between body size and tail size, the length of the wing in relation to the hook or any similar, seemingly minor detail.

It may follow that if an individual angler can spot one man's fly from another's, the fish can, too, if they're selective. They may be able to spot small differences in tying that can make the difference between whether or not they will take it. Perhaps that's why some anglers swear by certain tiers for particular patterns.

This is part of the mystery of why some anglers are more successful than others who seem to use identical tackle and to have equal skill.

Who is to judge a fly? I once overheard a pair of fly fishermen trying to decide who was the best fly tier in the country. One named a man whose fly heads were the smallest of all. He, therefore, considered that man the best. There is no question that a beautifully tied fly, like a technically beautiful painting, is a work of art. But one has to question if it is the technical aspect or the spirit that gives greatness to such works. Because the many materials of a complex fly are tied off at the head with the fewest turns of thread, is that fly better than one that has a studied carelessness and, as an imitation of a bug, seems almost alive? Or is a third fly, which looks pretty sloppy but catches more fish, better than either of the first two?

Most old-time fly fishermen have flies they love because of the sheer beauty of the design and workmanship. They love other flies because they have caught a lot of fish with them. Both fish and fishermen love flies, but not always for the same reasons. Should a fly be judged by the intricacies required of the fly tier or should the fish be the final judge?

I recognize and enjoy having flies that are beautiful both in my eyes and the eyes of other people. But when I go fishing I think of the fish as the judges of my flies, and I bow to their wishes. All the other parts of the fly fisher's art come into play while fishing. What value has a neat-headed fly if the motion a fisherman gives it seems fake to the fish? How well will a delicate dry fly work if it is splashed down in a tangle of leader too close to the fly line? Let us, when we go fishing, lose our hearts to the trout and let *them* choose from our ingenious imitations.

There is an endless variety of materials to choose from when making flies. In times gone by the British searched the world, taking feathers from everything from chatterers (blue jays) to bustards and making them into beautiful patterns. A fly tier soon falls in love with the endless array of materials that enables him to make as many as a thousand or more different patterns. The fly tier may experiment, as I do, and come up with flies that are new and different. Some he will like and some will not impress him. And he will fish hardest with the ones he likes best. If he's like I am, he will rarely tie one of a new pattern without tying a second to match it. I dread the thought of having a fly turn out to be successful, losing it, and not having a back-up pattern to continue fishing with or to copy when I get back to my fly-tying materials. A very few of these innovations become standard patterns, and the rest either continue as personal choices or drift into oblivion.

If a fly is good and catches fish and someone is impressed with it, the fly has a booster. If the booster is a tier he may make up some of the flies and sell or give them to someone else, and if they work for those who receive them the number of boosters grows. If there are people among the boosters with influence, such as outdoor writers or people who are vocal at fishing clubs, there's a chance the pattern will spread beyond the area of its origin. In the 1930s Jack Knight wrote an article about the Mickey Finn streamer, and, like a new song hit, it swept the country. Streamers, particularly bucktail streamers, were just coming into vogue at that time, and the Mickey Finn was a colorful fly with a colorful name. Most importantly, it really caught fish. Fly tiers were swamped with orders, and the fly became a standard.

Most standards, however, develop slowly, often with changes to the originals during their slow rise to popularity. Although a very ordinary fly can be promoted by publicity, it won't become or remain a favorite unless it has a reasonable amount of appeal to the fish it is supposed to catch. I can remember a number of red, white, and blue patterns that were sponsored by an airline or some other commercial concern. None of them made it, and the color combination seemed to mean a lot more to patriotic Americans than it did to the fish.

Sometimes a fly tier may get a few feathers that are attractive to him, but they are limited in number, and he isn't able to get any more. One day I found a young cedar waxwing that had fallen from its nest and died. The tail feathers were dark brownish with bright yellow tips. There were about ten of them, and I removed them before I buried the little bird. I used the feathers in flies that were beautiful and that caught trout for me. I had only enough feathers for five flies. When these flies were gone I tried to substitute dyed squirrel tail to get the same effect, but I failed. They did not have the special look I wanted. Either the trout, too, didn't like them as well, or I didn't fish them with the same faith as I fished the originals. The pattern died when I lost the last of the originals.

We should never forget that motion, either imparted to the fly or within the fly itself, may be the most important factor that leads a trout to strike. In the trout's view, if it moves it's alive, unless the fly or the motion seem fake. Matching the hatch successfully is glorious and failure to do so is disappointing. When we are having trouble let's always go back to square one and try to think from the trout's point of view. Is it hungry? If it is, what will tempt it? If the fish we cast over now doesn't seem hungry, are there others in the pools above or below that are? The essence of understanding angling is to recognize its problems and find solutions. Recognizing and understanding the problems is half the battle to success.

I was disappointed once when a fishing instructor, after conducting a complete course on fly-fishing for wild trout, sent his pupils out to his private pond to fish. He gave them no special instructions. If I had been the instructor, I would have said to the pupils something along the lines of: "Now you're going out to fish my pond. We've covered the stream insects and the flies that imitate them. Fishing always poses a problem that has to be solved, and the pond poses a special problem, in some ways different from those we've talked about but similar in other ways. These fish in our pond have been fed on pellets for the last three months, and you're more likely to catch them on something that resembles a pellet than something that resembles a mayfly adult or a mayfly nymph. But it's a very sophisticated sort of fishing, because these trout have been caught and released again and again. It should be fun. Good luck!"

Wild fish or tame fish have a very low order of mentality

compared to humans. It is true that they can learn to recognize that there's danger in a fly that has a leader attached to it or that a nymph with an unnatural motion can be dangerous, too. They can see the bend of the exposed hook and remember that the last time they took an insect with such an appendage they were in trouble.

The challenge for the angler—the problem—is not so much to outwit the fish as it is to cope with the fish's low mentality in a set of specific conditions. These conditions may include the trout's physical needs (is it hungry, satiated, relaxed, nervous?), the stream conditions, the types of food available to the trout and the trout's particular preference, if any, at the moment. Wind and weather are important, too. The sun may cast an angler's shadow that will scare the fish. The angler will want to use the wind to help him cast rather than to have it hinder him. The fisherman should know that a real grasshopper on a gusty day will hit the water with a splash—and his imitation should splash down on the water, too.

The angler should never forget that a fish, like a cat, is curious, but that the fish can also be easily frightened. The angler must avoid frightening the trout in his approach and presentation, and he must become a predator and think of his flies as living things to trick a lesser predator. Fortunately, man, in this day, can be a nonpreying predator, able to release his victim to give another angler a similar challenge instead of killing it on the spot.

Let us pull it all together when we fish. Let us love the flies we choose to fish with and hope the fish will love them, too. Let us do our best to recognize the problems that face us in fly-fishing, problems that exist not so much because the trout are wary, although that can be a factor, but because each day on each stream and pool offers a set of circumstances and conditions that are a part of the problem. In our minds, let us try to fit the fish and the fly we use and all the other aspects of angling into an overall picture, and then try to figure out what the fish's reactions will be.

We know that sometimes we will fail, but if we plan our campaigns well complete failures will be rare. Always we'll have the beauty of the fly-casting rhythms to give us solace and make the day worthwhile.

People are often surprised to learn that I hunt as well as fish. Most have known of me only as a fisherman. I enjoy hunting alone for deer when the woods are ghostly still, when the greatest skill and understanding are required. I also enjoy the sudden roar of a grouse that has been flushed and the shadowy target. And I enjoy both venison and grouse on the table. There is a difference to me between hunting and fishing, between guns and tackle. Guns are relatively simple. Since they were perfected, improvements have been few, but fishing tackle is quite complex and still offers great opportunities for innovation.

Give me a little time and material and I can enlarge the scope of the fishing world by improving the range of its tackle. I can design a line that will give me more casting control over a greater distance. I can work on rod tapers to give a better use of power for the particular casts I like to make. But, best of all, give me the materials, and I will come up with flies of new designs that will add to my chances of catching fish. Tying or buying flies is a year-round thing, and the choice of the fly, as much as anything else, is the secret to success and enjoyment in the wonderful sport of fly-fishing.

Index

Adams, 46
Alexandra, 47
Animal hair. *See* Fur
Ants, as bait, 40
Appearance, affecting effectiveness,
  21, 22, 24–25, 48–50

Bass
  flies for, 60, 73, 115–22
  saltwater, 128
Bergman, Ray, 16–17
Bivisible, 18, 49, 137
Black Gnat, 22, 47, 116
Black-Nosed Dace, 47
Blue Charm, 28, 132
Blue Dun, 32, 33
Bluegills, fishing for, 121–22
Bomber, 139
Brown Hackle, 22
Bucktail
  bug, 122
  use of, 18, 54
Bumble Bee Scraggly, 59–60

Caddisflies, 36–38
Caddis worms, as bait, 16, 17
Cahill, 32
Calftail, 54
Call-Mac, 118
Cicada, 40
Classes, fishing, 19–20
Coachman, 22, 140
Color, of flies, 28–29, 50–51, 80,
  134
Cosseboom, 134
Coty Stillwater, 71
Cowdung, 22, 140
Crazylegs, 95–96
Crickets, rubber, 24
Cullman's Choice, 134

Dark Montreal, 22
Devil Bug, 118
Doug's Darter, 100–1, 113
Dyeing, of feathers, 27

157

Effectiveness, factors affecting, 21–29
Entomology, need for, 42

Fat-Bodied Spider, 71
Feathers, for flies, 27–28
Flexible Hopper, 93
Flies
    basic assortment of, 45–51
    flexible, 85–99
    looped-hackle, 101–5
    materials for, 152–53
    plastic-bodied, 107–13
    Wulff, 53–62
Flies, dry, 24, 26, 46
    backward, 99–101
Flies, wet, 22–23, 26, 46–47
Floatant, 54
Fly-fishing, definition of, 147–48
Fur, use of 18–19, 54, 77

Glue, for flexible flies, 89
Gold-Ribbed Hare's Ear, 46–47
Grasshoppers, 40
    imitation, 48
    flexible, 92–93
Gray Hackle, 22
Gray Nymph, 26
Gray Wulff, 18–19, 26, 46, 48, 55,
    59, 117, 137–38
Green Highlander, 134
Grizzly Scraggly, 59

Hackle, for flies, 27–28
Haggis, 133
Hare's Ear, Gold-Ribbed, 46–47
Hatch, matching of, 31–44
    importance of, 42–43
Hendrickson, 32, 33
Hewitt, Ed, 17–18
Hitch, riffling, 133, 140–44
Hooks
    camouflaging of, 99–101
    sizes of, 86

Inchworms, as bait, 40
Insects
    terrestrial, 39–41
    water, 32–39

Irresistible, 53, 54

Jock Scott, 132

Kulik Killer, 78–79, 115

Lady Joan, 133–34
Leader, fineness of, 32, 64–65
Lead-Wing Coachman, 22
Line grease, Mucilin, 54
Looped-Hackle Hopper, 93, 101–3
Looped-Hackle Spruce Moth, 105,
    140

March Brown, 28
Mayflies, 32–34
Mickey Finn, 47, 153
Midges, 38–39
Midnight, 139
Minnows, imitations of, 74, 115–22
Motion, affecting effectiveness,
    21–24, 61–62, 77, 154
    in saltwater fishing, 128
Muddler, 44, 47
Muddler Minnow, 43, 46, 47, 81
Muskie, fishing for, 121

Nymphs, 47–48
    fishing with, 23–24
    flexible, 89, 94

Orange Fish Hawk, 22, 134, 140

Pale Evening Dun, 32
Panfish, fishing for, 121–22
Parmachene Belle, 22
Pens, marking, to color flies, 50–51
Perch, fishing for, 121–22
Picasso, 80
Pike, flies for, 120
Plastic-bodied flies, 107–13
Pliobond adhesive, 89, 93

Positioning, of fly, importance of, 32
Prefontaine, 67–68, 69–70, 138
Professor, 22

Queen of the Waters, 22
Quill Gordon, 15, 32, 33, 140

Rat-Faced McDougall, 140
RB Caddis, 17, 18
Red Ibis, 22
Retrieve, uneven, 23, 81
Rooster's Regret, 73, 117–18
Royal Coachman, 18, 22, 46, 47
Royal Wulff, 18–19, 43, 44, 46, 48,
    137–38

Salmon
    fishing for, 23
    flies for, 109–13, 131–44
Salmon eggs, as bait, 12
Saltwater fishing
    flexible flies for, 90
    flies for, 123–29
Sawyer, Frank, 27
Scissors, need for, 48–50
Scraggly, 59–60
Sea Wulff, 126–27
Silver Blue, 28
Silver Doctor, 47
Silver Gray, 132
Skater, 44, 48, 61, 63–71, 138
    for bass, 118
    tying of, 66–67
Skidder, 118–20
Spearing, of fish, 12, 148–49
Spent-wings, flexible, 90
Spider, 18, 25, 43, 44, 46, 48, 63–71
    fat-bodied, 71
    trimming of, 48–49
    tying of, 65

Spin-fishing, 149–51
Spinner stage, of development, 32
Squirrel tail, use of, 77
Stoneflies, 34–36
    as bait, 16, 17
    imitation, 17, 35, 46, 47
Streamers, 47, 73–83
    fishing with, 80–81
    flexible, 89–90
    shape of, 74
Stuart's Swimmer, 113
Sunfish, fishing for, 121–22
Surface Stonefly, 43, 44, 47, 70, 138
    plastic-bodied, 108, 109–13,
        134–35

Tarpon, flies for, 126, 127
Thunder and Lightning, 132
Tinsel, silver mylar, 116
Trout, brook, 22, 25
Trout, brown, 22
Tubes, flexible, 83, 85–99
    glue for, 89
    weighting of, 98–99
Tying, by hand, 13

Walleyes, flies for, 120
White Moth Scraggly, 60
White Wulff, 18–19, 60, 117,
    137–38
Wilder-Dilg, 118
Wilhold adhesive, 89, 93
Wings, of mayflies, 32–33, 60
Wooly Worm, 43, 44, 46, 47–48,
    136
Worms, rubber, 24, 86
Wretched Mess, 105–7
Wulff flies, 53–62, 137–38

Yellow Sally, 22

LEE WULFF was born in Valdez, Alaska, and currently resides in upstate New York near Livingston Manor. In almost fifty years of active writing and lecturing, he has achieved legendary stature in the angling world. Besides on many patterns, his name is in many angling record books; he holds the fly-rod record for striped marlin and the first tuna taken on sportfishing tackle in New-foundland. He is the author of six other angling books and has produced films about fishing for ABC's "American Sportsman," CBS's "Sports Spectacular," and many private and government sporting organizations. He is one of the founders of the Federa-tion of Fly Fishermen, served as a director of the Outdoor Writers Association of America and the American League of Anglers, and is chairman of the Atlantic Salmon Association. He has won the National Trout Unlimited Conservation Award, the Theodore Gordon Fly-Fisher's Salma Award, and the Winchester Out-doorsman of the Year Award.

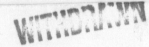